NEW SPACES
FROM SALVAGE

NEW SPACES FROM SALVAGE

Creating perfect interiors

from recovered architecture

Thomas J. O'Gorman

BARRON'S

First edition for the United States and Canada published by
Barron's Educational Series, Inc., 2002

Produced by PRC Publishing Ltd.,
8–10 Blenheim Court, Brewery Road, London N7 9NY
A member of the Chrysalis Group plc

All inquiries should be addressed to:
Barron's Educational Series, Inc.
250 Wireless Boulevard
Hauppauge, NY 11788
http://www.barronseduc.com

International Standard Book No. 0-7641-5407-9

Library of Congress Catalog Card No. 00-111164

Printed in China

9 8 7 6 5 4 3 2 1

Frontispiece: Signage with a decidedly religious theme, "Ave Maria," fabricated from white pine slats and Christmas lights, used in a Southwest United States festival becomes an electric wall sculpture in a contemporary interior. Beneath the glass table with stone pillar legs sits the letters of a contrasting electric sign with a less ethereal message, "PEEP."

Below: Cast iron window guard executed in a dragon fly motif reminiscent of the Art Nouveau style, from the Terminal Tower in Cleveland, Ohio, designed by the prestigious American architectural firm of Graham, Anderson, Probst & White in 1920. It is now used as a decorative element on the stairway of a Chicago Jesuit Prep School.

Contents

An Introduction

Remember that the most beautiful things in the world are the most useless.

John Ruskin

Above: Carved limestone Art Deco panel depicting the science of engineering, circa 1930, from the panels of the Ogden Avenue overpass in Chicago, Illinois. The panel is now part of the exterior ornamentation of the athletic center of a Chicago Jesuit Prep School.

Right: An urban loft; late 19th century American factory table with porcelain feet; 19th century French cafe chairs with remarkably distressed patina; Rococo chandelier with cherubs formerly used in Orthodox church. On the table, glass battery casing is filled with wooden glove forms from a glove factory.

Below: A 19th century French safe with original patina; pair of gilt bronze acanthus leaves from the capital of a Corinthian column; above on top of the safe are a pair of rounded iron finials; dull gilt framed mirror; and a 19th century English cast iron three piece decorative panel with classical Greek influence.

Have you ever been to a salvage yard, a reclaimed architecture center? If you haven't, you are really missing out on something big. If you have, well then you know what I am talking about. They are unique. Unusual. Kind of like a cross between a Hollywood prop department and an elephant burial ground. A warehouse of treasure. A strange environment. They are not your usual antique shop. Nothing demure here. Everything is big. The scale, the proportions, the stock, the artifacts themselves are big. A brawny atmosphere pervades the air, bouncing off the columns and steeples, the cornices of buildings, and the decorative chandeliers that hang like Christmas ornaments from the riggings overhead. A most curious breeze blows here made from the musty air of the past and the fresh air of the present.

Salvage centers are becoming more and more popular in many parts of the world. Their prominence tells you two things. First, there must be a market for all this stuff. And second, there must be something churning up all this loot. I suspect that few people notice the holes in the urban landscapes that teardowns and demolitions bring, and the chances are those holes do not remain for very long. "When we build, let us think we build forever," the aesthete John Ruskin implored his Victorian counterparts. Sadly, there is more poetry in his words than practicality. But long before the wrecking ball swings or the charges are set for the implosion, the household treasures and the architectural elements of another time are removed. And a seemingly endless supply of wainscoting, windows, doors, knobs, knockers, tubs, tiles, pediments, and pillars rise up in the figurative dust. Out of the destruction of the buildings of the past, many items of architectural value receive another chance at life. Ruskin would be pleased.

Italians have a favorite saying, *Tutto e arte*—"All is art." Such a panoramic view is their judgment on the vitality and the vibrancy of items of artistic merit. No wonder they jump-started the Renaissance. When all is seen as art, a dynamic spirit invades the intellect and eye. It sees beyond the surface value or purpose of a thing. Fueled with the imagination of the soul, such a view appreciates the fluidity of art, as well as its ceaseless ability to transform life. Here the eyes perceive the eternal romance within an object, the artistry that transcends utility. It validates the belief that objects of artistry are instilled with many layers of grace and beauty. Unraveling their many fibers of artistic meaning and purpose is the only sympathetic response to art. It emboldens the human mind with the ability to find the power and passion of art in many places. It is a vision of life that comes in very handy in the salvage yard.

It is easy to find art on palace walls, chapel ceilings, and the temperature controlled galleries of modern museums. However, a more resolute spirit is needed hunting for it in the back lots and loft rooms of salvage centers. Amid the rubble there, grand art hides. You can spot it in the carefully carved corbel or the graceful swirl of an Ionic column's capital. Maybe it is even harder to uncover,

laying off to the side in the crackled, peeling paint of a chair from a Parisian park—there is art in its sinuous form and in the generations of history that continue to cling to its frame. Art abides in unusual places, in the curving shape of an old wooden hat form carved by human hands. It is present in the battered finish of an old table that was purposefully created long and broad. Art jumps before you in the cast iron filigree of an antique French octagonal stove whose beauty warmed chilled hands and feet in another age. It is present in curving copper on a cornice whose shape came from the genius of an architect without rivals. In the whimsy of a French iron garden snake art that curls and coils like an evil subject from Eden. A walk through a salvage center is a passage through a museum without guards. All about you flow the remnants of artistic achievement stacked on tables and standing against the walls. It is a fingertip away.

Salvage centers can make you feel piratical. Walking among such treasure recalls the storage caves of Long John Silver, Bluebeard, and Captain Kidd. Strewed all about is the encrusted ornament of simple country life and elegant urban living. A ghostly flavor rides the air through room after room above the relics of another time and place. Some chimney pots and a garden gate might be all that remain of a once proud house. The stone steeples of an English country church are all that is left of a noble ecclesiastical shrine. Francis Bacon said that "Houses are built to be lived in and not looked at." I am not sure I agree with him. Perhaps he was of such simple tastes that ornamentation was outside his realm of appreciation. On the other hand, he might be rallying support for domestic disorder, finding purposeful design a needless affectation. In that case, England's eminent Elizabethan man of letters would probably go mad in a salvage yard.

Far left: A 1960s influenced modern interior. The burnt orange metal chimney funnel and the avocado green leather fireplace cushioned surround are almost emblematic of the period in color and shape. Contrasting is the 1920s cast concrete relief from the Prairie School, on the pebble-coated wall, from the studio of Frank Lloyd Wright by his assistant Iannelli. The sunken floor of this room can be flooded. Marble slabs serve as steps to the seating area.

Left: A pair of carved 18th century wooden brackets have been refashioned into a four-tiered bookshelf adding an ornate and dramatic focus within a bedroom interior.

"Architecture," Goethe, the German poet said, "is frozen music." Perhaps this is the mystery that leads man to see in stone and steel and arching wood things beyond the obvious. It is, I suspect, what has always been appealing about the shape and form that ordinary materials take on when fabricated by the order and symmetry of man's design. Beauty is further fused into nature with chiseled corbel, or unfolding marble acanthus leaf, or the minimalist curve of modern glass. Architecture shapes our environment and civilizes it. Having captured the aesthetic principles of nature, it further utilizes them to enhance the manner of our living in harmony and beauty. In every age, the eye of man has been shaped by the power of architecture, refined by its utility, and deepened by it practical awareness. In our own time, architecture is more than utility and function. The present interest in using architectural elements as ornaments of beauty and fashionable design is a

growing artistic phenomenon and a business one as well. People may not know the technical names of what they like, but they usually know what they like. Architecture speaks to deep down things. It is tactile, engaging, enveloping, and uplifting. It connects us to larger ideas and theories of grace and beauty.

Architecture has a deeply ennobling capacity to draw out what is richest and most human in man. It helps to bring order to the everyday chaos of living. Good architecture not only provides shelter and safety, it enlivens our shared experience of beauty and perfection in the world. It certainly did that for Thomas Jefferson and the founding fathers of the American Republic, who looked upon architecture as a vehicle for transmitting cultural integrity and enhancing the ideals of the nation. For Jefferson, the transforming power of architecture was best expressed in the traditions of antiquity. His passion

Left: Distressed mid-19th century commercial clock with Roman numerals, tin frame, face, and wrought metal hands. Used originally in an English factory, the timepiece is reborn as an object d'art and sits upon a table top in a contemporary setting.

Right: (Foreground) a three-piece terra cotta frieze of griffins and lyre; stone finials; (left) Welsh terra cotta pedestal and urn; English terra cotta sconce of stylized blooming vine; letter "Y" in Chicago terra cotta from the Broadway Strand Theater, Chicago; aluminum letter "C;" glazed French terra cotta urn; (background) cast iron window box; early 19th century cast iron vent; 19th century French cast iron valence; (right) pair of wood columns.

for Grecian temples and their arching domes and proportion, was a paradigm for larger issues of human civility.

When the movement to revive the treasured Gothic style of Britain's chivalrous past was first taking root in the 19th century, it did so with the belief that architecture in the style of the high Middle Ages would impart a piece of their heroic past again in the heart and soul of the British people. Gothic Revival was not just a trend or fashion, it was a way of life. It happened to come about at a significant juncture in the history of the British people. It is no accident that the splendid seat of their parliamentary government is designed in the style of its most noble and fabled past. Architecture is a dynamic art. All encompassing. It speaks what is most noble in us all.

No one knows exactly when the first collector reached out to reclaim a piece of architectural salvage. But there are plenty of instances throughout history when prominent figures, motivated either by taste, greed, or the need to retrieve a piece of the past, carried home some remnant of

appealing artistry and design. Just look at the Crusaders or Napoleon in Egypt or William Randolph Hearst in California.

By the dawn of the 15th century, it is said the ancient ruins of Rome were in such disregard that scavengers came from far and wide to remove its ancient stones. Some are even reputed to have been brought back to England for use in Westminster Abbey. During that period, when the youthful Filippo Brunelleschi, the architectural genius of Florence, traveled to Rome with his friend, the sculptor Donatello, it is recorded that they scavenged through the rubble of old Rome, selecting many of the choicest pieces for transport back home with them.

In the late 18th century, the second Lord Cloncurry returned to Ireland, following his grand tour of the continent, bringing with him two pair of splendid polished red granite columns taken from Nero's Roman Golden Palace, the *Domus Aurae,* using them to fashion a magnificent portico at Lyons, his grand country estate in County Kildare. His passion for reclaimed Roman architecture was unrivaled in Ireland, and even included remnants from the

Left: A corbel with hand-carved grotesque brings high drama to ceiling space with a very powerful piece of architecture that once adorned a Gothic Revival building. Its size and shape bring a stirring accent to this domestic environment.

Right: Four 19th century English Gothic Revival limestone church spires form a square within which are (from the forefront left) an English terra cotta chimney pot with cap and two chimney pots without caps, a limestone capital, a pair of American Victorian cast iron hitching posts, an English late Georgian carved stone sundial holding a French wire planter; (from the forefront right) 19th century French enamel cast iron stove, early 18th century English carved stone pedestal, Parisian iron garden snake (on right spire); (center) Second Empire French cast iron urn, decorative French iron garden pomes with stem and leaf, and assorted iron garden furniture.

Baths of Titus as well. In his front hall was a frieze of ox skulls and tripods from the Temple of Fortuna Virilis. Ancient architecture carried a romantic and erudite fascination for such exuberant personalities whose intelligent interest in architecture was only outdone by their financial where-with-all. They saw value in the ruined refinements and neglected ruins of the past and delighted in their ability to find new places for them in their more contemporary undertakings.

Nothing, however, expanded the possibilities of collecting such curious and eclectic additions to domestic ornamentation and decoration, than the massive expansion of the British Empire across three fifths of the globe during the heyday of the 18th and 19th centuries. Colonial service in the military or bureaucracy led to the acquisition by many families of items for display back home. At Curraghmore, the Irish country home of Lord Waterford, polo sticks were always kept in a stand made from the trunk of a

large Indian elephant. The Marquess of Dufferin and Ava, once Viceroy of India for Queen Victoria, is said to have carried off to his country house, Clandeboy, the sacred linen ropes that once lowered the Pharaohs of Egypt into their tombs. He hung them from the beams in his entrance hall where, recalled his great granddaughter, Lady Caroline Blackwood, they would flail the air during the night making a haunted and frightening sound.

In the picturesque English village of Wroxeter, in Shropshire, near what was once a Roman stronghold, the Church of St. Andrew's incorporates some Roman masonry into its construction. The baptismal font, there, is believed to have been fashioned from a Roman column. In Buckinghamshire, Sir Francis Dashwood, founder of the notorious "Hell Fire Club," built an extraordinary house called West Wycombe Park. This neo-classical estate he filled with architectural wonders from Greece.

Closer to the present, Chicago architect and metal worker Emil Pollack, whose technical artistry helped restore the metalwork of some of the city's most famous architectural masterpieces, like Burnham and Root's Rookery Building and Louis Sullivan's Chicago Stock Exchange trading room, now located in the Art Institute of Chicago, fashioned the giant revolving doors at the top of the Sears Tower. Mr. Pollak, over the years, became a well-known collector of antique revolving doors, taking great delight in their polished wood and fitted brass finishes.

Recently, at Greenwich Park, in southwest London, a curious excavation began in a paved-over area that once was the site of Montague House, the home of King George IV's German-born wife, Caroline of Brunswick. Workmen sought to uncover what was once Caroline's bath. Ironically, during her lifetime she acquired the reputation of seldom taking advantage of this facility, considered by many who knew her to be "malodorous." Great interest surrounds the possibility of unearthing this early 19th century tile-lined bath of the beleaguered consort of the foppish king who actually barred her from his coronation. The search adds credence to both the interest and technological possibilities in the present for uncovering such lost architectural remains.

Around the world, a passion has long abounded for the loot of the past and for utilizing the architectural elements of past history in the modern domestic design schemes of the present. Examples of such abound.

A gargoyle-faced stone pediment bearing a strangely familiar Hanoverian face, his powered wig and kingly nose blackened by centuries of English industrial grime, no longer presides from its cathedral niche. Instead, it rests now beside a fireplace in a cozy Chicago Gold Coast *pied-a-terre*, adding historic eminence to the room.

A sunset in balmy Malibu is framed within a neo-Gothic limestone arch, a refugee on the sandy California beach from its rainy Scottish border country origins. This stately folly has swapped its mid-Victorian pedigree now for more friendly winds and frames an ocean view.

A Regency mantlepiece, once the pride of upwardly mobile middle-class Londoners, now sits within the parlor of a meticulously restored Atlanta manse, adding its lineage and dignity to its even fancier modern owners.

Commercial art deco lighting sconces, once the glory of a Midwest movie theater in the roaring 1920s, have been recycled for domestic use and cast shadows now on the minimalist surroundings of a youthful urban dweller in a renovated Chicago candy factory loft. The gangster era patina of lighting is a wonder to his friends.

The garden gates of a grand Irish country house still swing from their ornate hinges, though they are a long way from the rolling hills of County Meath. They creak in baronial splendor still, in the front yard of the suburban American home of an orthopedic surgeon.

From the uselessly exotic to the prosaically functional, the materials and craftsmanship of the past are enjoying an exciting rediscovery in the present around the world. The fixtures, fittings, and objects of ornament—treasures, if you will, of "history"—are finding an unusual, yet contemporary second life. These relics of past eras of architectural fashion and design have found their way into the current realm of the modern and urbane, reshaping the domestic interiors of those who seek to *create the perfect space*. The stately remnants of old elegance are tilting the horizon of interior residential design. They might be the remains of a landmark home or the unwanted paraphernalia of an old hotel. They come from vintage buildings no longer economically viable, and from the renovations of stately governmental offices, cathedrals, basilicas, or old-fashioned theaters.

Left: A lush urban garden viewed from an upper balcony. The ground is covered in marble pieces that once made up the fascia of a well-known 19th century Chicago building, while the wrought iron staircase is thick with plants, complementing the black wrought iron garden furniture.

Right: 1870s Chicago Italianate domestic dining room with Georgian influenced high gloss pea green enamel walls and white lacquer windows and trim. The pine floors are hand decorated with a Greek key black and white design. The wooden capital with stylized leaf design, circa 1870s, is from Highland Park, Illinois, Town Hall and the 19th century American industrial hat form wall bracket with acanthus leaf motif, and Rosenthal china vase, date from circa 1915.

The origins and results of this explosion of the sale and reuse of architectural artifacts for home use is an intriguing tale that stretches from the salvage yards of Europe to the burgeoning artifacts markets and showrooms across the United States. In truth, the commotion in the salesrooms owes as much to the actual availability of imaginative and well-fashioned pieces of salvage as it does to the wide range of affordability in merchandise now available to buyers and weekend warehouse shoppers. People who once did not know an Oriel window from an Oreo cookie are fast becoming connoisseurs of rediscovered architectural salvage. Recovered architecture can be as simple as a chrome doorknob, as elegant as a stone column for use in a domestic garden, or as grand as a hand carved oak staircase that finds a second life in a modern home. A number of significant factors have helped to bring about the remarkable expansion in the market of artifacts.

First, a bright spirit of eclecticism—the mixing of styles that both contrasts and complements—is once again an element of popular taste, freely

Right: Frank Lloyd Wright dining room table and chairs in the Prairie School design are complemented by a hand crafted gilded silk screen by Wright and his son, for the Imperial Hotel, Tokyo; to the left is a Wright Prairie School chair. Above the room, suspended in front of a larger window are window panes made by the Wright Studio for a domestic residence. The wrought metal grate is by architect Louis Sullivan

encouraging the use of rescued items of salvage with artistic and architectural importance. For instance, French doors with a dusty 18th century legacy can gracefully combine with contemporary American furniture, Victorian mirrors, and tables of the Prairie School design. A mahogany bar from a saloon in 1930s Prohibition Era Chicago melds with leaded stained glass windows, once used in a German Lutheran Church, in an interior boasting a large brass chandelier that once hung in a French country house. The free mixing of such styles denotes a fresh appreciation for the rare and "one-of-a-kind." The subtleties flowing from the blend of these textures, materials, and surfaces create new and dynamic interiors. Elegance and whimsy can go hand in hand in the varied, and often unusual, juggling that these long-loved objects let loose. A strong sense of historic preservation becomes an abiding partner in this fashionable understanding of design.

Secondly, the availability in the present of lost craftsmanship from a more demanding time is an incentive in the use of architectural salvage. Often such elements provide an excellence in artistry and a quality of materials that are no longer available to the public. The forces of mass production long ago erased the high expectations of workmanship that were once a standard in

the not too distant past. Today, the excessive costs of fabricating from scratch such fittings for home use makes them available to only a select few. Reusing elements of the historic past, when both quality and elegance reigned, makes much more sense. Such preservation protects items of historical value while keeping home remodeling or construction costs relatively economical. The extra dividend is the intriguing and often romantic attraction to such quality.

Thirdly, a whole new resource for obtaining reclaimed architecture is today more readily available. From the shires of England to the rolling Highlands of Scotland, from the exotic cobbles of old Provence to the mansions of leafy New England, items of architectural design are being discovered for their artistic importance. Finials, classical pediments, newels, and balustrades, once the victims of the wrecking ball or dumpster, are being brought back to life by new applications of their design. With the discovery of a wide array of new uses, a more modern and distinctive character is being invested in them by discerning people. Ultimately, this is about style, tone, and, above all, *taste*. Architectural artifacts display unique human workmanship, most appealing to present aesthetic sensibilities. Remarkably, everything from door hinges to towel hooks, and fire grates to garden urns are reestablishing themselves as emblems of beauty, as they settle into new settings and environments. Designers shuffle the textures of fresh interior surrounds with the relics of the costumed past, establishing a neo-eclecticism that fits the modern passion for the romance of long ago.

Fourthly, in many American and European cities, an imaginative urban redevelopment is underway. Cities are coming back to life. In Chicago, New York, London, Paris, and countless others, the population of urban dwellers, younger and wealthier urbanites, is expanding. Old neighborhoods are being totally revitalized. A renaissance is underway. In the continuous search for new housing, the standard usage for many urban buildings is being transformed. Structures once used as factories or office buildings are no longer occupied for commercial purposes. Instead, they are being revived for imaginative residential use. Such settings offer more space than traditional apartments or single-family dwellings. The scale and proportion of many one-of-a-kind architectural artifacts is seen as tailor made for use in such reconstituted environs. They can help civilize and warm unusually large living spaces, adding, at times, touches of the wildly ornate to bleak interiors that are utilitarian by design. Elsewhere, they can offer sober restraint to areas of highly ebullient style.

New Spaces from Salvage seeks to expand the imagination and the creative risks of anyone interested in discovering new resources for shaping interior space. Your home, condo, co-op, townhouse, apartment, country house, or rambling period mansion can easily come to reflect your distinctive personality. Ideally, it will direct you to resources that will open fresh images of design. Farming the heritage of the artistic and architectural past is a convenient resource for dramatic domestic environments. The perfect space is not as difficult as you might think. Splash in an Edwardian bath, swoop down your own cantilevered staircase, snuggle up to a cozy hearth, shut out the noisy world with your own sliding Victorian pocket doors. It's as easy as a trip in the Winnebago to the mall.

In sprawling cities like Chicago, innovative salvage warehouses, such as Salvage One, bring the treasures of the past to customers from the best European and American sources. In New York City Urban Archeology has become the first name in artifact resource. Heritage, in Kalamazoo, Michigan, is fast becoming a popular Midwest site. Lasko, in London, and Wolcott's in the elegant town of Bath, are two of England's most sophisticated salvage centers. Their steady base of repeat customers is growing more architecturally savvy, attracted by their superb changing variety of stock. Whether you know the difference between a "broken" pediment and a "classical," customers learn best by a hands-on searching in the yards and warehouses stocking the treasures of bygone days. It is easy to acquire a comfortable working knowledge about the historical eras of architectural design and to learn the shortcuts to uncovering the examples that enable you to find that perfect piece of salvage for your home.

In part one, New Spaces from Salvage takes an in-depth look at those periods of style and fashion that continue to influence our tastes and appreciation for designs from the past in the present. From the Georgian fascination with the re-emergence of the Classical to the austerity of the minimalist's passion for the Modern, from the textured excesses of the heavy draped Victorians to the sinuous lines of the slinky Art Nouveau, interior design has ultimately sought to shape spaces for living. With high appeal to the senses, whether they are encrusted with the wholly artificial or free of every shred of it, simple objects of beauty and highly decorative ornaments of design have sought to make environments for man and woman in which they can feel more comfortable and at home. The lasting artistic expression of these eras of high artistry and fashion can still be recovered, complementing homes in the remnant artifacts left behind. This historical overview provides a valuable vocabulary and handy visual roadmap for traversing the salvage markets of the world.

A tour of the salvage yard with photographs showing how pieces can be put to work unfolds in part two. Learning the "ins" and "outs" of successful salvage hunting need not be a complicated endeavor. No one should be put off the search for that unique piece of reclaimed artistry because they fear they lack some special knowledge to help them through the task. What you find yourself drawn to, what you find appealing, is that which you should have. From piecrust tables to gazebos, from Corinthian capitals to four-legged bathtubs, from exotic pergolas to mirrored boudoirs, New Spaces from Salvage opens up the geography, language, and lexicon of treasured architectural loot from the past. It attempts to uncomplicate your passage through salvaged architectural treasures. It is an aesthetic voyage, a learning experience, a refresher course, and, most of all, an exhaustive approach to hunting out the best in human workmanship and what brings most enjoyment and satisfaction to your heart.

Developing a facility for uncovering that perfect item is the goal of this book. It may even make you an expert along the way. Short of that, it should make the process of hunting out architectural treasures exciting and satisfying. Certainly, you will become more interesting at dinner parties! Hopefully, you will be learning as you acquire a deeper understanding of how and where and what to acquire. If you discover some aesthetic pleasure, then we have successfully accomplished our goal. If you create your own perfect space, then you have used this resource well.

Creating an environment of beauty, tone, and taste, your perfect place—your home—should not be a difficult task, for in the end it is about that which gives life and restoration to the human soul. At least that's what the great English art critic and reformer John Ruskin believed as he attempted to affect the tastes and appreciation of his Victorian audiences. "Fine art," he was convinced, "is that in which the hand, the head and the heart of man go together." You couldn't ask for more than that!

PART ONE
Historical Periods

Anyone new to the hunt for really usable architectural salvage might easily find the wide variety of styles and designs available today quite complicated and confusing. Trying to keep straight all the various historical eras of architectural design can appear a daunting task. At first glance, all the period names and the nuances of variation within the different eras of history might appear overly technical and too burdensome to master. But nothing could be further from the truth. And while novice salvage hunters might not know all the differences between, say, the Georgian period of design and that of the later era of Gothic Revival, learning a few facts about how styles evolved and what political or cultural forces might have brought them about can easily broaden anyone's working knowledge.

With just a little attention to details, the key elements that go to define a particular period of architectural design can be at your fingertips. Knowing that the Georgians were neat and that the Victorians relished clutter can be of enormous assistance when wandering through an architectural salvage yard. Remembering that the glamorous flappers of the Roaring 20s were passionate for Art Deco and that hardworking American farmers brought about the Rural Style can quickly facilitate any search for period pieces of artistic design. Discovering the differences in the specific characteristics of period design should make salvage hunting both more interesting and rewarding. Taking the time to uncover the driving forces that brought about a particular period of artistic expression will aid anyone interested in learning how to better uncover artifacts of the past for use in interiors of the present. Learning a few key recognizable characteristics from each historical period of design can easily be accomplished. Acquiring a vocabulary that lets you speak with clarity and precision about what keenly interests you is not as complicated as it might seem.

In the following section, a concise thumbnail sketch of each relevant period of architectural design is intended to start you on that road to a good working understanding. From the 18th century to the present, every historic period demonstrates some unique artistic and cultural signature that identifies it. Recognizing the various shapes, lines, materials, ornamentation (or lack of it), as well as the intended function of an object or artifact from a specific period of design can become second nature, particularly when you give yourself the hands-on experience of rooting through some interesting salvage yards. The development and evolution of styles and tastes has always been a deeply human endeavor. What you will hopefully discover is an understanding of some of the forces of history that in every generation have been catalysts for change and development, as well as for the evolution of utility and the technology of design. The resulting reaction of one generation to the styles and tastes of another predictably stimulates new styles, new ideas, and new artistic expressions. Pay attention to those details. They can make you an expert.

Right: Note the simplicity and symmetry of the wood paneling of the fireplace surround, wall, and door of this early Georgian interior. Lighting is maximized by the multi-paned window. Furniture is both practical and well-made in the early Georgian manner, as is the glass decanter and glassware upon the table.

Georgian

Born and educated in this country, I glory in the name Briton.

George III

Right: An interior rich in detail of the middle period of Georgian design (1750s and 1760s), reflecting the period's passion for classical architectural design. The broken pediments above the entrance door and above the built-in wall cabinet display the linear symmetry of antiquity. The handsome tooled molding around the ceiling and the decorative carving on the fireplace surround demonstrate a growing interest in more highly elaborate decoration.

Below: A classical Georgian domestic residence. This very popular style of home is constructed in traditional red brick. Large windows, with eyebrow pediments above them, line the face of the house. The use of ironwork on the front railings, and on the second floor balcony, are a familiar feature of Georgian period style.

Corinthian columns and Roman temple designs. Greek palaces and stately linear shapes. Ornate plaster ceilings. Door cases with broken pediments. Cut glass chandeliers. Door furniture. The art of wood-turning is discovered affecting the shapes of balustrades. Custom houses and town halls built. Florid ornamental detail. In the homes of the well-to-do furniture becomes more comfortable. Grand houses, dignified public buildings, elaborate country homes, windows, chairs, and staircases of Classical perfection.

This highly creative and significant period of architectural design takes its name from four English kings named George. George I (1714–27), George II (1727–60), George III (1760–1820) and the Prince of Wales, later known as George IV (1820–30). The prince ruled from 1811 to 1820 as prince regent during his father's physical and mental incapacity.

This is a long period, 126 years, stretching, artistically, from Classicism to Rococo, from simplicity of style to the beginnings again of ornamental embellishment. In the 18th and early 19th centuries, the Georgian style of architectural design ushered in a new age of elegance, purity, and correctness in design. It marked the revival of the architectural style of ancient Rome and Greece. It was a natural transition in artistic tastes that has come to symbolize the Age of Enlightenment, the remarkable period of scientific, philosophical, cultural, and political reawakening of thought. The dawn of a new rationalism brought about a keen interest in the classical forms of the ancient past. A new sense of regularity was descending, bringing about new rules and principals in art and architecture. A new sense of restraint was developing as a reaction to the impassive uncontrolled turmoil of the Baroque style, which was an excessive confection of florid ornamentation.

This Georgian era demonstrated a return to the beauty of form and proportion, scale and harmony. This design, so influenced by the restrained antiquity of Rome and Greece, was expressed in the construction of many terraced houses for the middle class and landmark country houses for the aristocracy. It was a period of bubbling prosperity thanks to the vast colonizing efforts of the British government. With the arrival of the new king, George I, in 1714, as well as a new dynastic house of royal rulers, the German House of Hanover, politics in Britain underwent a considerable overhaul. During this period the Whigs, a political party of developing influence and power, gave their blessing and patronage to this new architectural style also known as neo-classicism. They appreciated the opportunity to distance themselves from all the excesses of the past. The ornate embellishment of Baroque architecture and the overblown politics of their parliamentary predecessors were jettisoned in favor of their new sobering political influence and the new artistic designs that recalled the nobility and ideals of Rome and Greece.

The early decades of the 18th century saw a renewed interest in things Roman and Greek as many well-to-do English people traveled to Italy and Greece on what they called "the grand tour." On this journey they came face to face with an artistry with which they had little previous experience. What they discovered was a welcome change from the whipped-cream-like excesses of 17th century styles. In England, the Earl of Burlington, a man of high influence and large wealth, became so enamored with the architectural writing of the 16th century Italian Andrea Palladio, that he published his writings back home in English. It was a big boost for architects and fashionable people of wealth and position. They joined the Earl in their admiration for this exciting new architectural style. Palladio was heavily influenced in his work by the writings of the Ancient Roman architect Vettruvius who described the intricacies of Roman artistry. In addition, archeologists during this period had just unearthed the lost city of Pompeii. Its discovery captured the imagination of many civilized people and further highlighted the rage for elements from antiquity.

Palladio's designs recaptured the splendor of both Rome and Greece and produced five kinds of classical motifs or orders that became the hallmark of all neo-classical design—the Tuscan, Doric, Ionic, Corinthian, and Composite forms. Architects influenced by him produced a style of architectural design that excited the growing new moneyed leaders in politics and commerce. It proved to be a powerful antidote to the excesses of the past. And this remarkable style had a dramatic effect on both public and domestic building endeavors as well.

Among the more intriguing elements of Georgian style was the heavy emphasis of the symmetrical grand façade that often incorporated classical columns into their design. Pilasters and balustrades also helped to detail the shape of this new linear fashion. Domestic architecture became rectangular with a new incorporation of windows that gave integrity and balanced scale to exterior designs. The use of sash windows came into vogue, and the Palladian window or Venetian window rising above the front door also became an important feature of the influence of classical principles on Georgian architectural design. Ornamentation was curtailed to the simple application of classical detail such as antique shell motifs, acanthus leaves, or scrolls. Dramatic porticoes reminiscent of ancient Rome became an important feature of Georgian neo-classical architecture, demonstrating the newly acquired simplicity of taste for classical symmetry and proportion. Doorways, porticoes, and windows were now flanked by stately columns. Materials such as polished woods—oak or pine—were used to build doors of proportion and noble scale. The geometric principles of architecture and design that so fascinated and intrigued the Ancient Romans and the Greeks were reawakened in 18th century England. Georgian architects came close to matching the ancients' artistic excellence and grace.

American Colonial and American Federal

Yankee Doodle came to town,
A-ridin' on a pony,
He stuck a feather in his hat,
And called it macaroni.

Dr. Richard Shuckburgh

American Colonial—two story timber house, log cabins, Chesapeake dugouts, Dutch influenced Hudson style, red brick Queen Anne. Salem, Massachusetts. Williamsburg, Virginia.

American Federal—neo-classical, Georgian, temples, a sturdy and abiding patriotic tradition. Columns, gabled roofs, mullioned cornices. Solid paneled shutters flanking windows. Deeply American. Mount Vernon. Monticello. Cambridge, Massachusetts. Newport, Rhode Island.

This period of design is broad geographically and historically. It stretches from what is essentially the dawn of the colonial enterprise in American New England. American Colonial reaches from the first simple colonial experiment in Jamestown, Virginia, and continues up to the high complexity of colonial refinements of 1776, when colonists declared themselves free from British rule. The American Federal period roughly corresponds to that of the Regency in England.

The arrival of the Puritans in Massachusetts, in 1620, set in motion another sustained experiment in colonial living. From "New England" would arise the spirit and ethos of colonial life. From the outset architecture in the colonies centered on what was practical—especially in light of the harsh northern winters. From the Puritans, a religious sect that sought to live free of excess and clutter in both religious and social life, a sense of quiet refinement became an abiding part of the American landscape. Early English settlers in America carried the ethos of Tudor England with them

and often it was reflected in the structures that they erected. Around 1720 the beginnings of the neo-classical style were first introduced from England and after this, styles reflect the turgid tide of 18th century American colonial politics. It is a period that corresponds to the Georgian period back in England. This style portrays the experience of the New World settlements. Like the everyday life of the colonies themselves, there is a built-in practicality encased in this style. For example, many fine woods were available in the colonies and they were utilized to enhance the beauty of colonial homes. But life was more rough-hewn than in England, so there was little time for the extravagances or the excesses that were more readily available back on the other side of the Atlantic. Little idleness could be afforded in the colonies; individuals prospered due to their observance of a creed of hard work. In spite of this, those colonists familiar with the refinements and the beauty brought by the revival of classical design in England, sought to imitate the style in the American colonies. It was a style well suited to the fresh way of life and with adaptations to the peculiar materials available in the colonies, whole cities sprang up in this colonial Georgian style, a reflection of both local tastes and advancing colonial fortunes.

Following the success of the colonial revolution and the establishment of the American republic, this style became more peculiar to the ethos of the new nation's independence, and the term "American Federal" more accurately defines the thirteen states' penchant for elegant architecture. It was at one and the same time pragmatically "American," in its necessity and its freshness. Boston, Charleston, Philadelphia, and, of course, Washington, D.C., reflect the influence of this style of design.

Rural Style

If you want people to think well of you, do not speak well of yourself.

Blaise Pascal

Right: Rough-hewed and rustic was the heart of the rural American style. It represented a high moment in the craftsmanship of the folk-style. A simplicity and functionality that civilized the wilderness, this was design with roots in the religious traditions of many European cultures that rejected ostentation and lived in partnership with nature.

Below: Rural America produced a uniquely practical style that demonstrated the refined tastes and abilities of America's agrarian culture. Saltbox simplicity echoed a deeply romantic expression in domestic design that carried over to other homestead structures. The white picket fence is an icon of American domestic style.

Simple, handcrafted design. Functional agrarian living. Bare, elemental, essential environments. Handmade implements for domestic use stressing economy and efficiency. Quilts, rocking chairs, weather vanes, screen doors, white picket fences, barn board, farm tables, butter churns, clay jugs, iron stoves, iron skillets, pie safes, stills, and linen chests.

America's rural character was the making of the nation's settlement. In the 19th century homesteading permitted many Americans the opportunity to leave the more highly populated areas of the country and receive land parcels for farming in return for relocation in the more sparsely populated areas of the West. As immigration to the United States increased, the expansion of the continent and the richness of farmland were both attractive and practical to many large groups of rural Europeans.

Many of the nation's best farming communities had their roots in the various evangelical religious communities that left Europe for new lives in the heartland of America. Many such religious groups exercised austere lifestyles, eschewing the trappings of modernity for a counter-cultural expression based on religious principals. Among the better known were the Shakers, Amish, and the Mennonites.

The Shakers settled in rural New England shortly before the time of the American Revolution. What they lacked in external ostentation, they made up for in a clever and ingenious inventiveness. Their homes echoed their humble choice of communal, celibate living. At the same time, their work ethic and originality helped to produce furniture and utilitarian artifacts that seemed reflective of the New World spirit. Perhaps they are best known for the unusual type of cast iron stove that came to bear their name. Because it was the religious practice of the Shakers to assemble for prayer standing around the four walls of their homes and literally shaking as a religious style of prayer, they developed the custom of having four legged stoves free-standing in the centers of their rooms. A clever but elaborate chimney pipe ran just beneath

their traditionally high ceilings for venting and exhaust. In addition, they developed the unusual practice of hanging their simple spindled furniture on hooks around the room to give them more room for religious devotions. Their furniture was lightweight enough to easily permit rooms to have many functions, while reflecting the needs of farmhouse living and colonial American resources. Their brand of practical, communal living is also reflected in the long tables that bear their name and which permitted large groups to break bread together. The Shaker style had a heavy influence on popular tastes.

The Amish are a religious sect arising out of the German evangelical movement of the 19th century, practicing restraint and harmonious agrarian living. Their farms, largely in the fertile region of Lancaster County, Pennsylvania, are noted for their excellence in design and in their sturdy homemade traditional craftsmanship. Even today, the Amish reject the use of modern conveniences like electricity, the automobile, and mechanized farm equipment, preferring instead to hold on to a way of life grounded in simple living through which they find deep spiritual meaning. Amish simplicity centers on utility and lack of material clutter.

In addition to these deeply religious communities, the heartland of America produced an enormous agrarian culture whose commitment to rural simplicity became an esteemed way of life from the Prairie to the Rocky Mountains, from the cornfields of Iowa to the dusty hamlets of the Southern tobacco plantations, and from the dairy farms of Wisconsin to the fertile hillsides of New England. This culture produced sturdy furniture and a tradition of well-made domestic interiors that reflected this essential American way of life. The harsh realities of farm life developed a style of rural artistry that was evocative of country living. Distressed furniture, well-crafted homemade artifacts, hand-made quilts, cookware, crockery, barn board, screen doors, hooked rugs, front porch swings, hand pumps, washboards, and oil stoves, all reflect the details of utilitarian rural life.

Regency

Hail glorious edifice, stupendous work!
God bless the Regent and the Duke of York!

Horace Smith

Mirrored glass, linear plaster moldings, yellow, crimson, pinks, and gold popularized as fresh colors; pelmets, tied-back curtains, built-in bookcases, Greek and Egyptian motifs, crystal chandeliers, and oil burning table lamps. Simplicity. The Age of Elegance. Delicate decoration. Evolution in furniture—Hepplewhite and Sheraton—often gilded, with animal head and leg supports. Chandeliers become popular and mirrors are often used to line the walls of interiors to brighten available light.

Though the Prince of Wales, the Prince Regent, only officially ruled in place of his father from 1811–1820, his influence upon this style that bears his name began late in the 18th century and continued up to the beginning of Queen Victoria's reign in 1837. It represents a period of style and fashion as much as it does a political era.

This is the era of Jane Austen novels, Beau Brummel's fashions, and the Brontë sisters. Convex mirrors were all the rage, gilded, and often embellished with stately eagles. Cast-iron kitchen ranges took cooking to a new level of convenience.

More simplified Georgian, the style is typified by suburban gentility and plainer interiors with less ornamental plasterwork, as well as simpler architectural detail that some see as a prefiguration of the Art Deco movement. Color became more important in interior styles. The strongest influence came from the Greek revival that is displayed in distinctive motifs like the Greek key pattern. Bowed fronts and bayed windows become popular. Houses are smaller. Stucco came to be used in exterior design. Cast-iron canopies, balconies, verandas, and porches also came into use.

Hooded windows with balconies were popularized.

Symmetry, elegance, and proportion are all the signature of the Regency style, together with representations of the classical Greek and Roman ornamentation. Beauty in form and proportion.

Ancient Egyptian based themes—palm trees, sphinxes, and the like were popular in both the French Empire and the English Regency—and derived from the military actions taken in Egypt during the Napoleonic wars. The urn and swag motif became a popular style in the domestic embellishment of fireplaces. Tombs, furniture, and buildings exhibited the urn motif as well.

By the turn of the 19th century, the Industrial Revolution further brought about new technological

advances in the production of ironwork. This is the era of great engineers and great feats of engineering such as suspension bridges. Seaside resorts grew in popularity during the Regency period. They were laid out in crescents, squares, and sea-front terraces. Windows, often running floor to ceiling, permitted maximum opportunity to enjoy the sea air. Architect John Nash became well known for his Regency terraces and houses. In London's Regent Park, built in 1810, we have his most elegant expression of terraced city housing.

This style takes its name from the period that coincides with the incapacitation of King George III. From 1811 until his death in 1820, the King faced with serious physical and mental problems was unable to function as king. His oldest son, George, the Prince of Wales, who later would become

King George IV, took over the role of day-to-day head of state. The Prince of Wales' influence, however, began about twenty years before he became regent. It is also a period that coincides with the rise and fall of Napoleon in France and the wars that raged across Europe because of him on the on the Continent. The style was very much influenced by the tastes and patronage of the Prince Regent, as he was known. Its refinement has its origins in the French Empire style made popular under Napoleon. It began in England as a style done in admiration of the French.

In the decorative arts porcelain flourished both technically and artistically. Wedgewood led the way in high porcelain artistry. Later, it was followed by Bow, Derby, Chelsea, and Worcester. Spode, Copeland, and Minton followed after that. English pottery of extraordinary refinement.

American Greek Revival

I am a citizen, not of Athens, not of Greece, but of the world.

Socrates

The ultimate American style. The Acropolis on American soil. Columns and capitals. Classical temples. Domes. Banks, cathedrals, and courthouses. The unembellished frieze. Pedimented porches. Proportion and symmetry. Geometric design. High accomplished engineering. The antebellum plantation house. Rational. Geometric. Vaulted interiors. Simple porticoes. Small classical clapboard homes. Gables. Pilasters.

The Greek Revival style of architecture was a popular genre of American architecture beginning in the early 1820s and lasting up until about 1860, roughly the start of the American Civil War. This architecture was inspired by the beauty and elegance of Ancient Greece. It is familiar to many because it is the style of countless banks and courthouses across the nation. But it was a style heavily employed in domestic architecture as well. Across the American South many wealthy plantation owners chose Greek Revival as the style for their signature country mansions. Remember Tara and Twelve Oaks? Greek Revival design. An impeccable grandeur and refinement easily flows throughout this style. Undoubtedly this is why Thomas Jefferson, one America's earliest and most distinguished architects and patriots, chose Greek Revival for his own Virginia country estate known as Monticello. He also selected this style for his creation of the University of Virginia in Charlottesville. Jefferson led the way in helping to popularize this architectural style, often adding his own unique embellishments to them. When he was supervising the design of the United States Capital Building in Washington, D.C., he insisted on adapting the classical form of its Greek Corinthian columns by substituting leaves of American tobacco and corn for the traditional acanthus leaves, demonstrating symbolically the manner in which this style could further make itself a part of American life.

By the 1820s, the American Republic was an infant no more. Its stability and growth emboldened its character and Greek Revival architecture was a natural form to express how the nation and its robust democratic leaders perceived the future of the country. They saw in the architecture of Ancient Greece, the original birthplace of democracy, the perfect paradigm of American greatness. In addition, many people tired of the heavily used Georgian style of design that had been so identified with the country's former ties to Britain. After the War of 1812, Americans had little liking for things British. Something new was needed. Something fresh, demonstrable, and innately adaptable to America's growing grandeur.

It is no accident that the builders of many public buildings found the style so engaging. These classical façades and porticoes echoed stability and high ideals. They bespoke confidence and trust. In America, finance and justice found a comfortable coziness within the temple-like forms of revivalist construction. An added feature of the movement was the remarkable development that took place during this period in the quality and execution of engineering features. As the nation became more and more engaged in industrialization, the leading professional architects of the

Right: This American Greek Revival interior expresses the American passion for the refinements of classical architecture in the mid-19th century. The elaborate fireplace surround with ornate broken pediment and carving is the anchor of this New World refinement. Many great houses along the rivers of the continental interior made this style the nation's most popular.

Below: The dramatic classicism of the American Greek Revival period became emblematic of the antebellum period. These classical Corinthian columns and pediments shape a balconied portico that expressed both an affluence and refinement in which Americans took great delight.

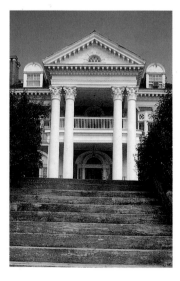

movement advanced the science of American engineering with remarkable technological precision. Among the more eminent proponents of the style were Benjamin Latrobe who executed the South Wing of the United States Capital, and William Strickland, Jefferson's mentor and the designer of the Parthenon-like Tennessee State Capital.

Greek Revival proved to be a very successful form of domestic architecture on a more modest scale as well. Across the nation, applications of the Greek style began to dominate the tastes of regular folk. One reason for this success was the introduction of pattern books published by revivalist architects. These works contained the architectural plans pre-drawn for general use. Asher Benjamin, author of the highly influential *American Builder's* Companion, blueprinted popular instructions and became the foremost guide for Greek Revivalism, making the intricacies of the engineering and design readily accessible through these very popular works. Builders across the nation could now use the patterns to fashion Greek Revivalist homes. Soon the familiar features of the style—classic clapboard exteriors and bold simple lines—became the most popular housing style in the country.

Greek Revival style had established itself as a unique expression of American ideas and democratic self-awareness. It was a crowning achievement and became a distinctly American style from Virginia to Mississippi and from Boston to the expansive reaches of the American frontier.

Second Empire

The last time I saw Paris, her heart was warm and gay, I heard the laughter of her heart in every street café.

Oscar Hammerstein

Gingerbread-style of house. Mansard roof, dormer windows, classical balustrades and pediments, elongated windows often featuring pilasters or columns on either side, arched windows, projecting and receding surfaces, ornate, elaborate wedding cake-like design. Bay windows, cupolas, towers, and verandas, all influenced by Italianate design. Elaborate chandeliers and floor lamps. French Renaissance style. Italian Renaissance style.

French Victorian? Perhaps. An amalgam of styles? Certainly. In 1848, Prince Louis Napoleon, nephew of the infamous French emperor, managed to get himself elected President of the Second Republic and eventually this Prince-President maneuvered enough politically to have himself declared Emperor of France. The Second Republic became the Second Empire. Napoleon III, as he styled himself, began to reshape the politics of France and in the grand tradition of his family, proceeded to reshape the city of Paris itself. Much of what the world knows today as the elegant cityscape of boulevards in the French capital was redesigned under Napoleon III's influence and his ever-watchful eye. Often extreme measures were used to clear out tenements and erase old unsanitary alleyways across the city. In the Bois de Boulogne, for instance, the Emperor had two lakes dug to reduce the inelegant level of urban dust. Many parks, straightened streets, large squares, and fancy buildings unfolded in this extraordinary undertaking.

Corresponding to the mid-decades of Victorian design in England, the grandeur of this period of French architectural influence saw the construction of showcase governmental and commercial properties—the Paris Opera House by Charles Garnier is a good example of the high style that emerged under the Emperor's influence. Though Napoleon III sadly ended his days in exile following France's disastrous defeat by Germany in the Franco-Prussian war in 1870, the grandeur of French architecture remained and flourished. Grandeur was the underpinning of the design style that attempted to translate the sense of French national pride into stone and masonry. The Emperor saw himself as the inheritor of his uncle's legacy, as well as the royal guardian of French taste. His lavish court life necessitated the introduction of a high style that had long laid dormant in France.

The telltale features of Second Empire style—elongated boxy shapes, steep double-sided mansard roofs, dormer windows, towers, rounded cornices, classical pediments, bay windows, and balconies—quickly spread to England where they proved very popular. (Both the Paris Exhibitions of 1855 and 1867 were influential in popularizing the style.) But, however fashionable it was in England, it was nothing compared to how enormously popular it became in the United States. In Washington D.C., the new Executive Office building constructed during the Presidency of Ulysses S. Grant, was done in the Second Empire style. In Philadelphia, the new City Hall erected during the nation's centennial celebration, was fashioned in the Second Empire style. It was a richly expressive style that denoted authority and classical elegance, which fit the self-perception of the United States during one of its most prosperous periods of affluence. It soon evolved to a very successful style in domestic architectural design too, being considered progressive and modern. With the American Richard Morris Hunt, who had studied at the Academie des Beaux Arts in Paris, the leading proponent, Second Empire seemed ready made for the needs of the nation's expansionism, and many homes as well as great public buildings were built in the fashion. In the northeast of the nation in particular, Second Empire proved a bestseller. The familiar mansard roof filled the quaint towns of New England as small town America rediscovered sophistication in this exotic "French influenced" fashion. The popularity of this style was enhanced by its practicality. The mansard roof and dormer windows had a great utility, providing an expanded use of attic space. So popular was it that the style almost seemed to be an American original, it certainly transformed the character of many small towns. These houses were the quintessential expression of small town American refinement.

With the coming of industrial machine-made elements for use in the decorative arts, the exteriors of Second Empire buildings were often richly enhanced. Such details seemed to lend themselves to the lifestyle of the late 19th century. Large wrap around porches permitted family members and neighbors to socialize in large scale comfort. At the same time, their elaborately exuberant Gothic qualities, particularly when in distressed conditions, lent themselves comfortably to countless tales of fright and horror as the perfect setting for haunted terror.

The Second Empire style proved to be a popular and dramatic style that fit the tempo of late 19th century American living as well as it fit the glorious aspirations of French nationhood. Using the most modern advances of the industrial age, this fashionable yet utilitarian design was an important expression of late 19th century bourgeois values and urban respectabilities.

English Victorian

I will be good.

Queen Victoria

A new ornateness. Fringes. Tassels. Dark woods. Wallpaper. Red brick. Ornamental iron work. All these details announce the transition to a new taste and design. A heroic and inventive period in history and in domestic and commercial design.

In 1837, the granddaughter of George III, a slight, but graceful eighteen-year-old girl, succeeded her uncle, King William IV, as the British monarch. Her name would resound throughout the remainder of the century as the epitome of British might and authority. Known to the world as Queen Victoria, she would preside over a period of unprecedented prosperity and invention, setting the standards for propriety and taste until the end of the century and her death in 1901 at the age of eighty-four. Her influence was without equal, arranging for many of her children and grandchildren to occupy most of the thrones across Europe. Her name gave itself to an age of discovery, an era of refinement and a sturdy style of architecture, design, and living encrusted in the exotic and the urbane. During the reign of Queen Victoria, the very function and purpose of architecture itself underwent enormous change. It could do so because of wide technological advances that expanded the possibilities for the age. It was during this period that something as simple as factory-made bricks came into being, not to mention electricity, the elevator, the postage stamp, the indoor toilet, photography, and macadam roads. Nothing demonstrates the Victorian style more than the heavy use of those familiar red bricks. Building in this material was economical and efficient and helped to shape a familiar urban architecture. The large-scale need for such new materials was necessitated by the expansion that occurred in cities across the globe. London, New York, Chicago, Paris, and Prague are just some of the cities that underwent unprecedented growth.

This was also the age of iron and steel. The development of such materials during this period led to new ideas in how buildings could be fashioned and how high they could become. Wonders in engineering symbolized the era. Not only did iron bridges help to alter man's ability to harness nature, but also the development of the steam engine and its application to rail and water changed the ability of people to travel.

The advent of industrialization in the early decades of the 19th century created a new class of rich, those who made their fortunes from their own efforts. This "new money" often felt the need to impress others in the complex layers of the English class system. Their new wealth permitted them to build new and elaborate country houses, as well as impressive town houses. From the varied

Right: This cluttered interior is symptomatic of the Victorian taste for overwrought decoration. Bric-a-brac rests everywhere. The screen, pianoforte, walls thick with paintings, and the excess of furniture display the period's fancy for eclecticism and collecting.

Below: This baronial English Victorian country house is typical of the widening fabrication of such luxury mansions during the era of vibrant mercantile success. The achievements of the middle class were often celebrated and advertised by such spacious and extravagant country homes. The red brick and gabled rooflines are emblematic of the bold style that emerged in the Victorian period.

tastes and exotic colonial fashions which became popular in Britain new genres in both exterior and interior style arose. Faux-Egyptian or neo-Elizabethan proved popular styles in which new immigrants from the working-class sought acceptance by their newfound success.

The expansion of the British Empire through Africa, India, the Far East, the Middle East, the islands of the Caribbean, and the Pacific exposed those at home to new and exotic cultures. Such influences led to the development of a highly eclectic period of style. It was pure pastiche. The clean and simple lines that for so long symbolized the influence of the neo-classical style was eclipsed by the rich and textured clutter of Victorian heterogeneous designs.

The Victorian period is so expansive that within its almost seven decades, a number of architectural developments spin off into new sub-sets

of architecture and design. Wide diversity prevailed and the Victorians mixed styles with impressive success. Tudor would be juxtaposed with Moorish, Regency accented with Indian and the medieval. Victorian interiors were lush and tactile, celebrating the age and designed for coziness, the needed respite from the industrialized age. And domestic living was going through an evolution as evocative as the one of which Mr. Darwin wrote. Gone from new homes were the great hearths of the previous Georgian era that burned tree trunk-like logs. Instead because of the more common use of coal, plentiful in the period, fireplaces in sitting room and bedrooms were reshaped. They could be smaller, more decorative, and usually, in the Victorian age, cluttered with the familiar signs of domesticity—mirrors, photographs, ornamental vases, and other knickknacks.

American Victorian

What is conservation? It is not adhering to the old and tried, against the new and untried.

Abraham Lincoln

Pocket doors and overwrought newel posts. Bric-a-brac, heavy draperies and dark woods. Tall ceilings, fretwork and clutter. Stained glass windows and medieval designs. Gothic revival detail, gas lamps, glass globes, fringe, lace doilies, horse hair furniture, machine made items, mass produced objects of interior design.

The period known as American Victorian, corresponding roughly to the last half of the 19th century, was a stirring and exuberant era in the life of the United States. It encompassed both the tragic years of the Civil War and the large-scale destruction of the affluent life of the American South and the geographic expansion of the nation across the continent. It was a time filled with grandiose commercial accomplishment and industrial expansion, as well as achievements in scientific and technological affairs. From the old settlements of New England, Americans moved out across the plains and the prairies reshaping the geography of the nation. Discoveries of large deposits of gold and silver in the western territories of the country brought excited people in large numbers hungry for the possibility of new wealth. Many were successful. In cities like San Francisco, Carson City, and Denver wildcat fortunes unearthed the building blocks of a fresh civility and boom in the development of new urban refinements. Millionaires roamed the streets and fashioned enclaves of luxury reflecting their remarkable success. This was the era of the transcontinental railroad, when the vast reaches of the continent were connected by iron rail. The bridging of the east to the west brought new settlers, new development, and the construction of new cities and towns. Everywhere people looked, America was expanding. This post-Civil War period was one of great wealth and optimism. America had reached the milestone of a century since its independence from England. and the country had a lot to be excited about. Manifest Destiny, the claiming of the whole North American plain from ocean to ocean, was an intoxicating and long-held dream. It was now coming to pass. The nation demonstrated its unique democratic achievement and the lasting reality of the Republic at Philadelphia in 1876. There, visitors gazed with interest upon the dramatic fashions of the day, especially the stylings of Charles Eastlake whose Hints on Household Tastes and other Details, became the bible of American domestic interior design. His popularization of mass produced items stimulated such industrial design and brought it to homes across the nation.

Below: The exterior of this residence denotes the adaptation of the Victorian style in American design. Clapboard siding, multiple eaves and gables, wrap around porches, centralized chimneys, and a dramatic scale of proportions represent the bold achievements of American Victorian design. There is an almost foreboding shadow about the house.

Left: This American Victorian interior demonstrates the fascination with the ornate. Heavy wood furniture was usually stuffed with horsehair, the over embellishment of the window treatment has an exotic quality to it. The harp expresses the era's delight in home entertainment. The extravagance of the carpets portrays the great luxury that was a part of the period's excess. Lamps and chandelier have crystal teardrops that further embellish.

Modernity was the rage in this era. Stylistically, a great shift occurred in popular tastes. As the nation celebrated its industrial success, those with the financial ability to build great houses did so in the new fashion. Revivalist architecture was all the rage. Queen Anne, Gothic Revival, Italianate, and the East Lake School were all appealing expressions of the fresh fortunes of many Americans. They no longer looked to the tired styles of the past, like the Greek Revival and the Neo-classical that had been popular before the War. In the styles and trends of popular fashion, Americans also celebrated the new inventiveness of the age. They did things because they could. The rise of industrialization brought about the widespread use of machine made goods. The ability to reproduce architectural forms and items of intricate design by machine unleashed a elaborate exuberance in design. The ability to "mass produce" enabled outlandishly ornate and intricate styles to abound. The fancier the better, became the ethos of the times.

This was a time of eclecticism and clutter. A hodgepodge sense of style in domestic interiors was a calculated rejection of the simple life. Large fortunes begat complicated tastes. Those wildcatters who made their fame in the West, looked to the gentility of the East to make them both stylish and respectable. And while today we might look to this era of overdone excess as garish or tres mooch, the reality back then was just the opposite. This was a dramatic expression of the modern. Modernity arose every time a machine reproduced the same balustrade over and over again. Modernity reared its proud head every time a machine replaced a craftsman in the repetitive duplication of a piece of architectural design. It was cheaper, faster, and more dependable—hallmarks of modern American living.

A powerful break with the past came in the excessive striving to be fashionable during the era of American Victorian styles. Ironically, in the generation to follow, the children of these fortunes and fashions would openly reject these overstated tastes and go running back to the sublime restraint of the Neo-classical. When they sought to create a style to express their inherited wealth, they would reach to the precedence of the historical, finding in the crisp lines and regal simplicity of the Georgian period a style of higher aesthetics and understated elegance. Ironically, when the World's Columbian Exposition opened in Chicago, in 1893, celebrating the 400th anniversary of Columbus's voyage of discovery, Chicago architect Daniel Burnham chose to design the buildings of this world's fair in the Neo-classical style. He sounded the death knell for this overindulged and exuberant style. The modern had moved on.

Gothic Revival

There was a knight came riding by
In early spring, when the road were dry;
And he heard that lady sing at the noon,
Two red roses across the moon.

William Morris

Gargoyles and traceries. Spires, flying buttresses, vaulted ceilings and crokets. Monastic influenced with arches that seemingly point to heaven, thanks to the absence of a keystone. The romantic touch of the medieval. In reality, a style of architecture that began in France and spread across Europe between the 12th and the 16th centuries. Gothic revival is most familiar to us today in the countless churches and college buildings that appear to have been built in the medieval past, but rather are instead the product of 19th century romanticism. They symbolize a striving for the age of chivalry and high romantic ideals.

Toward the end of the 18th century, a romantic fascination with the medieval led to a renewed appreciation of the merits and elegance of its design, in which a dramatic sense of perfection was perceived. Its stunning manipulation of stone and its curious ability to send such weighty material soaring toward the sky deepened the period's attachment to the emotionalism and spiritualism found in such intrinsic beauty. By the start of the 19th century, architectural tourism to the great symbols of Gothic construction—like Chartres, Rheims, and Notre Dame de Paris— flourished, brought about by the publication of new research into the details of medieval living.

Below: A renewed interest in the design aesthetic of the Middle Ages expressed itself in the architectural style of mid-Victorian tastes. Here that noble form is demonstrated in stone. The arches of doorway and windows portray the tracery style of medieval.

Victorian romanticism ripened under the shadow of its allure. This sturdy ecclesiastical style spoke to those who saw the Middle Ages as a proud era in human civilization, inspiring people to lofty ideals. It seemed to symbolized an epic era of achievement and Victorians found in it the perfect style to symbolize their own ideals and new perfection. As Britain sought mastery over the globe by their own unique brand of elevated imperialism, here was an architecture that was worthy of their unique status as masters of the world.

Nothing helped to advance the popularity of the Gothic Revival more than the decision to rebuild the Houses of Parliament, following a disastrous fire in 1834, in the Gothic style. The Palace of Westminster, designed by Sir Charles Barry, along the River Thames, stands as the pre-eminent expression of Gothic Revival in London. Its placement so near Westminster Abbey, a true masterpiece of 13th century English Gothic design, is almost a bow before its poetic splendor. The remarkable detailing of the buildings of Parliament were nearly all produced by A.W.N. Pugin, the architect whose genius almost single-handedly led to the revival of Gothic design. Many country houses displayed not only the wealth of their owners, but their passion for the baronial feel that came with their almost fairy tale look. When Queen Victoria chose a design to memorialize her late husband, her beloved Prince Albert, in Kensington Park, she selected Sir Gilbert Scott's spired Gothic masterpiece as her eternal remembrance. Tower Bridge, by Barry and Jones, erected over the Thames in 1894, perhaps best displays the marriage of the medieval with the Victorian. Its two impressive Gothic towers, so familiar to people around the world, in actuality are far more functional than would seem at first glance, concealing the steel framework for the bridge's support.

During this period drawing rooms came to resemble church sanctuaries, domestic holy of holies. Embellishments and ornamentations were straight out of medieval times. Heavy wooden furniture, often of mahogany and giving the appearance of a throne, was nestled beneath quatrefoil niches, or beside suits of armors and weaponry that created the haunted feeling of a past age. Windows bore the telltale imprint of tracery design, those ornamental mullions and transoms at the top of Gothic windows. Castellated roofs, chevrons, and faux battlements and arrow slits were soon replacing the Neo-classical columns and classical orders of design from the previous century. Clerestory windows, high in the area near the ceiling of a high room or hall, brought light into the interiors of Gothic houses.

The Gothic Revival carried a powerful influence in the Victorian age. It displayed a sturdy sense of power and authority that was a comfortable luxury for the developing barons of industrial success and achievement. In the class-conscious world of Britain, it enabled everyone to have a taste of palace living and fortress domesticity. In public architecture, particularly churches and museums, like the Victoria and Albert, the revival of Gothic design transmitted a sense of self-assured nobility to any who needed to know Britain's place in the world.

Right: There is an almost ecclesiastical quality to this Gothic Revival dining room. While the style is from the Middle Ages, the highly polished woods are strictly Victorian. The heavy, almost weighty character of the furniture, the leading of the window glass, and the excess of baronial wooden embellishment brought a sturdy pride from England's past to the Victorians.

Arts and Crafts

Everything's got a moral, if you can only find it.

Lewis Carroll

Right: This Arts and Crafts interior expresses a profound simplicity in its use of warm polished woods. The wood itself has become the artistic motif throughout this home. Accented with Persian carpets, there are no other aesthetic distractions. The room demonstrates order, reserve, and an uncluttered style.

Below: This Arts and Crafts imprint, common in wallpaper design and stenciling, has all the ethereal naturalism that flourished in this "return to basics" movement. This motif, made popular by William Morris, added a refined simplicity to domestic interiors.

A "back to basics" movement. A holistic approach to architectural and interior simplicity through excellence in handcrafted design. This was an artistic reform movement that prefigured the development of the modern through its attempt to simplify. Setting new standards of beauty and a more studied attention to quality in design and craftsmanship were essential factors in its success.

The Arts and Crafts movement was chiefly concerned with restoring simple tastes to ordinary people and providing them with well-crafted objects of design that reflected such tastes. This was essentially an aesthetic movement that began in Britain during the second half of the 19th century as a reaction against the excessive embellishments and clutter of the Victorian tastes. The heavy use of ornamentation in domestic interiors, and the proliferation of cheap, poorly-made objects that emerged for consumer use through mass production, were perceived by the movement's proponents as betrayals of the ideals of art. The beginnings of the movement were also a reaction against the everyday excesses of the Industrial Revolution itself, with the resultant loss of human spirit. The shoddy quality of workmanship in mass-produced objects underscored the need for reform.

In Britain, the leaders of this artistic movement were prominent painters and poets like John Ruskin, William Morris, Edward Burne-Jones, and Dante Gabriel Rossetti. They had already come together in a group called the Pre-Raphaelite Brotherhood to purify painting, returning it to the spirit of art that flourished in the Middle Ages, or at least as they romantically believed it had. To them the Middle Ages was an era of high ideals, lush natural beauty, and high moral endeavors. It represented a fragrant world of the past excellence, long before the advent of belching furnaces and smoking chimneys of the industrial age.

The architect A.W.N. Pugin shared their love of the romantic simplicity found in the medieval and became an influential proponent. He translated its aesthetics into elevated edifices of vaulted stone, building countless churches and public edifaces across Britain. To the leaders of the movement, a certain nobility of spirit was seen to pervade these buildings reflecting the age of the medieval. In the rich but simple details of the medieval, a powerful force of artistic renewal was expressed—a call to honesty in craftsmanship and romantic beauty in design. Architecture, furniture, and the decorative arts would be highly influenced by this movement.

Simplicity became the driving force of the movement, stressing handmade workmanship that expressed quality in every detail of design. In addition to a heavy medieval influence, exotic Oriental imagery was also a pervading influence. It soon found itself a style in high demand. The Arts and Crafts movement indulged in a heavy use of wood and wooden boards in interior design. Barrel-vaulted ceilings. Hand-painted friezes. Floral wallpaper, with almost tapestry-like motifs, deeply

the movement, going on to become its most important salesman. His hugely popular book, Hints on Household Taste in Furniture, Upholstery and other Details, had a far-reaching effect on the public. In many ways, he became the "Martha Stewart" of his day. His advocacy of a simple, unifying style, encouraging honesty in the way things were constructed and finished was a breath of fresh air. He altered popular tastes. When his book was published in the United States in 1872, it became the decorator's bible.

The influence of Ruskin, Morris, and others soon had a significant effect on the development of the Arts and Crafts movement in the United States as well. There too it developed as a reaction to the strong sense of stylistic eclecticism (clutter) found in the overwrought embellishment in the decades that followed the nation's Civil War. In the simplicity and the hand-wrought quality of furniture, interiors, and domestic necessities, Americans saw the paradigm of their own national origins. It was an appealing aesthetic. The medieval, however, did not offer the same attraction to American tastes. Instead, they were more affected by the splendid use of heavy grained woods and the simple interiors they fashioned.

In America, the Arts and Crafts movement found fertile ground in which to take root and flourish. Proponents of the movement reshaped the contours of American living. Gustav Stickley, enamored with the work of Morris and Ruskin, went on to establish the first truly American furniture known as Craftsman. By the turn of the century, his influence on American tastes could be measured by his success at bringing handcrafted furniture, imbued with the simplicity and honesty of the English Arts and Crafts leaders' ideal, into the homes of American families. In Southern California, brothers Charles and Henry Greene developed very popular homes and interiors reflective of the Arts and Crafts aesthetic. In New York State, Elbert Hubbard was heavily influenced by Morris as well and spread the doctrine of Arts and Crafts through his book design at Roycroft Press. He also turned out decorative items, metalwork, and Mission-style chairs and tables.

In a later generation, the work of the famed Scot architect and designer, Charles Rennie Mackintosh, bears the grand imprint of the Arts and Craft movement. In a similar way, in America, Frank Lloyd Wright would carry the same principles of simplicity and craftsmanship into his highly inventive style.

The Arts and Crafts movement was very much a reaction to mass-produced furnishings that appeared so poorly made. English aesthetes, designers, architects, and craftsmen set in motion an important and influential movement that would continue into the 20th century.

It was a rebellion against the loss of quality and beauty, function and form. It marked a rejection of the ornate, uncomfortable, and unfunctional furniture of the Victorian style. Simplicity, and the use of natural elements of beauty, were the prescriptive cure. It was a time in which light literally could stream into the dark rooms of Victorian shadows, through the widening windowpanes of the Arts and Crafts movement's influence.

influenced by the hand of William Morris, ripened with the use of pre-Renaissance imagery such as roses, medieval beasts, birds, lions, and exotic vines. Stenciling and hand-painted design-motifs also became very popular in domestic interiors. So too did wooden casement windows and bay windows. Fitted furniture, built directly into walls, changed the feeling of domestic interiors and occupied an important place in arts and crafts design. Window seats, inglenooks, bookcases, cabinetry—all had a practical dimension to them as well as beauty, helping to minimize the unnecessary clutter of Victorian living. At the same time they added a cozy layer of warmth, comfort, and charm. Doors too developed renewed significance in the Arts and Craft house. Their shape and design became heavily influenced by various historical periods—medieval, Tudor, Elizabethan, Byzantine, and Georgian—adding beauty as well as durability.

Charles Locke Eastlake, an English architect and writer, who was heavily influenced by the work of Morris, went beyond being an adherent of

The Prairie School

A little sincerity is a dangerous thing, and a great deal of it absolutely fatal.

Oscar Wilde

Pure American. Human scale and proportion. Low pitched roof. Long horizontal form. High windows and indirect light. Simplicity and harmony. Wood and stucco exteriors. Organic architecture. Interior designs reflecting the exterior design. Simple materials in buildings and in the furnishings. Architects Frank Lloyd Wright, Walter Burley Griffin, Marion Mahoney Griffin, and George Grant Elmslie are among its greatest proponents. Absence of excess ornamentation and decoration.

The Prairie School as its name denotes was intensely reflective of heartland America. If it called to mind the flatlands of the Midwest and the harmonious spirit found in abundance on this fertile expanse, then it had done its job. This was American architecture and design in its most exalted expression. It was America's only original architectural style. No influences from the historical periods or revivalist trends of European styles could be found in it. It was pure 100 percent American.

The origins of this unique American expression of design developed at the turn of the 20th century in the studios of Frank Lloyd Wright, perhaps America's most famous architect. Having worked in the Chicago firm of architect Louis Sullivan, the Wisconsin-born Wright participated in the unique development of the Chicago School that Sullivan and Daniel Burnham effectively set in motion in the last decades of the 19th century. From his suburban studio located in Oak Park, Illinois, Wright created a style of architectural design that was both uniquely modern in its conceptualization and surprisingly domestic in its application. Wright developed a style that was tailor made for the landscape of the Midwest, reflecting its sobering elegance and intense American self-awareness.

Right: This Prairie interior is replete with the telltale hallmarks of the Frank Lloyd Wright school. Narrow brickwork on the fireplace, the rich use of wood, the horizontal line created by the wood molding, the light fixture, and the leaded windows all bespeak the master of Prairie design.

Below: This Prairie style house has a decidedly Asian feel to it. A low, angular roof treatment gives the design a long feel. The height of the windows permits maximum privacy, but also maximum natural light within. There is a dramatic modern sense to this design style.

Wright gathered around him a talented group of young architects in what developed into a highly imaginative studio-school. Among his most talented assistants were Marion Mahoney Griffin and Walter Burley Griffin. Advocating an intense simplicity of design in both exterior and interior development, Wright created domestic architecture that was a "lifestyle" as much as it was a unique type of home. His interiors reshaped domestic living spaces. His aesthetics strove to create a harmonious and holistic environment that was intensely modern. His nine principles of

architecture were an attempt to rethink the way human beings cohabitate. He streamlined interior spaces and scaled everything to appropriate human size. His ceilings, set at a height of eight feet for domestic design, created a homescape very much in touch with the realities of human living. He eliminated the familiar box shape of interior rooms and created a flow within that was sensitively human. By placing windows high in his walls, he maximized available natural light, but set the activity of living beneath the prying eyes of street traffic and pedestrians. This enwrapped people in an interior design that was made soft and warm by the use of wood beams and wooden furniture, also of his design. Even basements and service elements such as heating apparatus were an intrinsic part of the harmony of his interior design.

Wright homes around the country all enjoy special celebrity. Among the more well-known are his 1901 Frank W. Thomas House, his first in Oak Park, Illinois; Robie House, built in 1907 near the University of Chicago, and considered the best example of the Prairie style; Taliesin, his home and studio school, built in 1911, in Spring Green, Wisconsin; and Fallingwater, the last Prairie influenced home built for Edgar Kaufmann, in 1936, in Mill Run, Pennsylvania.

Wright's influence cannot be under estimated. Derivative styles echoing his linear simplicity and bare-bones domestic influence can be seen in the suburbs across America. Though many of these track housing communities lack the quality, grace, and grandeur that Wright espoused in the later concept for cheap suburban homes that he called Usonian, his vision of a need for homes of modern utilitarian design was both inspired and imitated. Any American "ranch-style" home in some way owes its shape to Wright's idealism.

Ironically, Marion Mahoney Griffin and Walter Burley Griffin, a husband and wife architectural team who met in the Wright Studio, won an international competition in 1914 to design the new Australian capital of Canberra. They designed it in the Prairie School style, exporting this singular American architectural expression to Australia, and expanding Wright's influence in the process. It is interesting to speculate on the reasons why Australians found the style so attractive. Not least, certainly, must have been the harmonious simplicity and utility on which both Australians and Midwesterners place high value.

The down-to-earth style of the Prairie School has had a lasting impact on American life. Wright and his followers enriched the landscape of America, from the Midwest to California and from Florida to Arizona, with a style that was as practical as it was inventive, reflecting the heartland character and values of American life.

Art Nouveau

Today when something is not worth saying, they sing it.

Piere-Augistine De Beaumarchais

Organic. Sinuous. A movement initiated fully fledged by Victor Horta in Brussels in 1892. Metal shaped like vines from the trunk of a sapling. At the Paris Exhibition of 1900, public attention was centered on Art Nouveau structures that were the talk of the event. Art Nouveau interiors as fantasies of design.

The Eiffel Tower. A sensuous decorative style extracted in part from the heritage of French Rococo. Good examples are the familiar vine-like station façades of the Paris Metro entrances. Maxim's well-known restaurant. The Tassel House, Brussels.

An important 19th century program of renewal in architecture was realized in this rather short-lived movement, which can be seen as the first stage of modern architecture in Europe. Rejecting historical architectural styles, it was a reaction against the popular trends of the end of the Victorian Age. As a style Art Nouveau was concerned with appearance rather than with function, and was brought about by advances in metal construction during the decades that preceded it.

Mixing styles that included the baroque, oriental, and classical, its floral designs of lily, the iris, and the orchid are reflective of its preoccupation with living organisms. Stylistic representations of undulating plant-like contours of nature—leaves, flowers, dragonflies, peacocks, swallows, and swans are often seen, as is the female body and long flowing hair.

The basic elements of Art Nouveau were the muted colors used ("greenery-yallery colors, such as lilac, lavender, sage green, olive, and mustard"), along with glass and light. Under the influence of English painter/poet William Blake—especially in the graphic design elements of Art Nouveau—the movement turned away from the eclecticism of the times and exulted in the profusion of the irregular, curving linear ornament inspired by plant life with its constantly curving surfaces.

Its origins were in France and Belgium where Art Nouveau flourished in the last years of the 19th century up to the start of World War I. Blossoming out of the famed avant-garde movements it was a reaction to the academic and historical point of view and offered a highly

Below: This Parisian "Metro" station entrance is the very symbol of Art Nouveau design. There is a fresh modern feel to the shape and form. Even this most utilitarian of entranceways in urban public transportation has an organic, ethereal style.

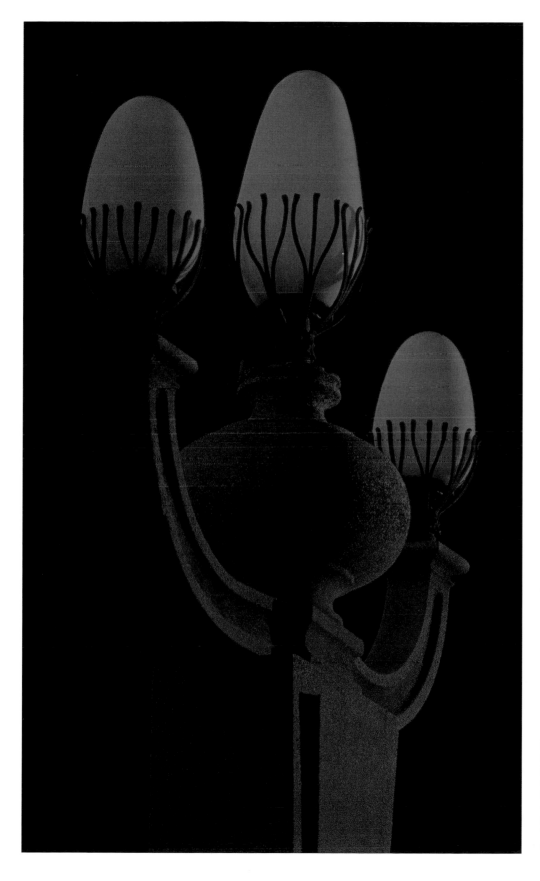

decorative style, emblematic of what the French called Le Belle Époque—"the beautiful era," as the last years of 19th century life were known. A distinctive style of architectural detail and decoration, it soon spread its stylized wings and became fashionable throughout Europe and to a lesser degree in Britain and the United States. In Scotland it was characterized by elongated rectilinear forms; in France and Belgium by flowing curvilinear elements; and in Britain and the United States by a combination of the two. Most of this work was purely decorative. In Scotland this was more angular through the work of Rennie Mackitosch and Mackmurdo. In America the work of the designer Louis Comfort Tiffany owed much of its curious exoticism to Art Nouveau. His glass curtain for the National Theater in Mexico City was directly influenced by the movement.

Chicago Architect Louis Sullivan, however, was America's main expositor of Art Nouveau. His decorative orna-mentation is almost Celtic in its intricate interweaving forms and there are many points of comparison between Sullivan's ornate metalwork and that of the Europeans, like Horta. Sullivan's Chicago skyscrapers were a doorway into the origins of modern architecture. a

Left: This composite concrete lamp in the Art Nouveau style expresses the fusion of modern form and function with the graceful shape and texture found in the high elegance of the period. The modern use of electricity in city life was enhanced by the refined style and gave artisans new opportunities for quality design.

Edwardian

I must get out of these wet clothes and into a dry Martini.

Alexander Woollcott

Right: These elegantly simple casement windows, express by their leaded panels a style and design of historical proportions. They permit a grand vista over the rolling countryside. The built-in furniture is another mark of warm Edwardian interiors.

Below: This remarkable English country house design by Sir Edward Lutyens is notable for its grand use of red brick that effects a sleek angular style that is visually captivating. The great chimneys add a powerful but refined sculptured linear perspective. This building is all shape. Pure simplicity. Its organized style is the height of the Edwardian ethos.

Simplification in interior design. The reduction of clutter. Less bric-a-brac and heavy decoration. The enhancement of domestic interiors with comfortable furniture. Less formalized domestic design. The popularization of the built-in window seat. The automobile and telephone find a wider popular use.

The sixty-four year reign of Queen Victoria came to an end on January 22, 1901. She had occupied the throne since 1837—a long period of political, technological, and artistic change. Her own personal standards of reserve and an unflinching sense of private decorum were not reflected in her heir and oldest son, Edward VII, who as the long suffering Prince of Wales lived life in more boldly social and scandalous pursuits. He had little time for the staid conventions and stuffy middle class satisfactions by which his mother had ruled a large portion of the known world.

Edward was a man more at home with pretty courtesans and horse racing than the pursuits of home and hearth. Fancy food and the high life were much more the preoccupations of this heir to the British throne who was permitted little involvement in the day-to-day governance of his mother's kingdom. It is no wonder that he was better known for his contributions to the worlds of fashion and cuisine than to the politics of his age. It is said that his impatience with the formal eveningwear of white tie and tails resulted in the creation of the first "dinner jacket."

So it is not unusual that he would lend his name to the emerging design and fashion popular at the turn of the century and which would would last until the dreaded start of the Great War of 1914. The Edwardian era was a time of revivalist historical styles. Like the new king, the style of the times recoiled from the clutter and eclecticism of the Victorians. Not only was there a new monarch, there was a new century. It was a natural juncture for the convergence of styles and tastes. English Tudor was one such fashion that returned, along with the appetite for English and French Neo-classicism.

A restraining air graced the arrangement of design at the start of the 20th century. In domestic interiors, both paneling and wallpapers were used with renewed effectiveness during the Edwardian period. Practicality, that very un-Victorian aesthetic, reared its head again, along with a renewed interest in personal comfort. Furniture began to become softer and less formal, going so far as to

actually support the physical comfort of its user. Edwardian instincts were best demonstrated by the creation of a relaxed sense of coziness—rooms and houses were designed to let in the best interior light, especially through those generous windows that were often leaded, beveled, or tinted. A studied reasonability flourished throughout Edwardian design, blending a more subdued feeling into domestic design. Though largely a continuation of Victorian style, it was greatly cleaned up, touched with new invention, and imbued with the ethos of a new century.

The Edwardian era was an awakening after the long Victorian sleep. The world was stirring to a new sense of modernity. Electricity was reshaping the everyday lives of ordinary people, though many were still dependent on the use of gas and candles. The automobile was further changing the way people traveled, though horse and buggies still plied the city streets. It was a period caught between the old and the new. But as people looked ahead to the future with sincere excitement, they also had the ability to savor the classic historical periods of the past.

No one demonstrated the renewed freshness and clarity of Edwardian manners and design more than the architect Sir Edward Lutyens. His grand country houses portray red brick exteriors of remarkably clean lines featuring a scale of refined domestic proportions that appear both highly modern and thoroughly expressive of the historic past. Vague shades of Tudor regality were toned down for modern livability. His work contained strains of Arts and Crafts beauty further strengthened with a sensitivity to nature. Lutyens, and the Edwardians in general, expressed an attentive harmony with nature that was the underlying spirit in their work.

The Edwardian era demonstrated a refinement and tastefulness that was conscious and appealing. There was a timelessness about its emboldened sense of what was fashionable. The modern was germinating in everything. As the curtain fell on the era, so did the catastrophe of World War. Nothing would ever be the same again. Huge cultural and social breaches arose out of the stirring events of the war, making the Edwardian era perhaps the last gilded moment of the old world.

Modern

Beauty is like a rich stone, best plain set.

Francis Bacon

The corporate high rise, utilitarian, rectilinear. "Bare bones." 20th century minimalist design. "Less is more." Technical monochrome character. Visual simplicity. Glass and steel construction. Flat, crisp industrial lines. Metal and leather furniture. Absolute simplicity of design form. No embellishment or external ornamentation. "Form follows function."

The roots of modern architecture and its expression in a coherent, unified artistic design can be seen rearing its head back in the last decades of the 19th century. It was then that proponents of the Arts and Crafts movement and adherents of the principals of Art Nouveau struggled to find expression as well as beauty in the modern principles of simplicity and functionalism. They attempted to develop a style of architecture that could lend itself to the evolving necessities of the industrial age. New technologies and the proliferation of inventions added to hunger. Modern architecture in America first was born in Chicago, when the method of steel frame construction was developed and buildings could rise high and slender, no longer dependent upon ponderously thick masonry walls to support the tremendous weight of their multiple floors. This multi-floored construction was a perfect form for urban commercial needs. In a limited space, workers and commercial enterprises could expand up rather than out. Nothing, with the exception of the invention of the elevator, so transformed the development of modern high-rise construction as this element of design.

Modern architecture's most influential proponents have hearty international roots. The German school of modern design developed by Walter Gropius, known as the Bauhaus, was an incubator for some of the most significant architecture of modernism. Unpopular with the Nazi movement, Gropius and others, such as Ludwig Mies Van der Rohe, came to the United States in the 1930s, leaving behind in Germany a body of work that became known as the International Style. Each of these architects would deeply influence the direction of architecture in America and around the globe. At the same time, in France, the architect known as Le Corbusier introduced the world to a new and exciting, urban form of functionalism with the use of concrete in his heavily industrialized design. These Europeans from early in the 20th century had set

Below: This home was created in the high design of the modern school made fashionable by Mies Van der Rohe. Basically, it is a glass box framed by black cordon steel. A design originally used in multi-storied urban settings, this country house permits extravagant unobstructed views of the landscape.

Right: The high utility of this staircase demonstrates key features of the modern school of design. The compact shape of the stairway, the use of minimalist metal railing, and the simplicity of its form all express a commitment to the ultimate function of the staircase.

out to develop new solutions to ever increasing problems that came with industrial living. City planning was a critical issue in Europe before World War II. In a very short period of history, Europeans had evolved from an almost medieval peasant-like way of living to one that was centered on an industrial or technological base. Industrialization changed the face of Europe. So architects set out to resolve some of the conflicts ordinary people faced in everyday living, like where to live and what to live in. New possibilities in construction were tested and more functional forms of design in residential housing were critical, given the constriction of available space in many old cities. New solutions were a necessity.

After World War II, the work of these architects flourished in many American cities. Building skyscraper apartments, single-family dwellings, and important commercial high-rises, the face of America underwent considerable changes beginning as early as 1948. At that time, Mies Van der Rohe designed two twenty-six story apartment buildings on Chicago's Lake Shore Drive that would become emblems of his black steel and glass construction. In New York City, his Seagram's Building, begun in 1954, continued to challenge old tastes and sensibilities. Le Corbusier, at this time, was part of a design team who fashioned the headquarters of the United Nations along the East River in mid-town Manhattan. In 1950, Gropius designed the Harvard Graduate Center in Cambridge, Massachusetts,

introducing his industrial style into the heart of Harvard life. In rural Illinois, Mies Van der Rohe set Farnsworth House, an early domestic masterpiece, began in 1946, on the flatland of the Prairie. It is still acknowledged as a house "ahead of its time." The well-known American architect Philip Johnson, a disciple of Mies Van der Rohe, along with countless others, carried the dramatic ethos of the modern school to new levels of expression and refinement. His own home in New Cannan, Connecticut, known as "The Glass House," because of its walls of glass set between black cordon steel mullions, bears the imprint of his life with Mies Van der Rohe and remains stark, simple, and full of expression in the lush Connecticut countryside.

Today, the work of the modern school has grown into an important part of most American cities. What was once so challenging and conflicting to ordinary tastes has gone on to become a part of our everyday life. The genius of the modern school brought about a style of architectural design that reflected the needs and lifestyles of their own age. The austerity and lack of decorative embellishment that is so expressive of their work demonstrates a new capacity for engaging the workplace and its environment. An enlivening practicality was at the center of their work. It sought to simplify the complexity of life in the techno-industrial age that soon became the atomic age. Modern architecture and artistic design were tailor-made for the complexity of urban living.

1950s—Mid Century Modern

You ain't nothin' but a hound dog.

Elvis Presley

Rock and roll. Television. **Big** new cars. Road signage. Motels. Suburbia. Track housing. Shopping malls. Juke boxes, drive-ins, bowling alleys, and soda fountains. Household appliances and consumer products. Modernist design in domestic architecture.

The use of atomic energy ended World War II and changed the world and popular tastes forever. Popular American culture expanded to extravagant proportions. Necessity and practicality brought about the development of a highly functional, basic domestic architecture with a new simplicity and restraint in exterior embellishment and ornamentation. It heralded the rise of suburban living. Families retreated from the nation's cities in large numbers. A boom arose not only in domestic construction, but in the need for schools, churches, and public buildings as well. Sleepy small towns grew into sprawling suburban developments overnight. The fast-paced development brought about a preference for a new "modern" style and rejection of the tired styles of the past. America was creating its own look in the 1950s. It was a substantial part of its new self-perception as a leader in the Cold War.

Everyone has different perceptions of the 1950s. It was a provocative and unusual era in both the history of the world and in the history of architecture and design. For many, the attraction today is the fascinating popular American culture, owing much to the coming-of-age baby boomer generation. The nostalgia created by television reruns and retro sensibilities from that period are also strong factors. The population explosion occurring in America in the 1950s produced a culture focused on family and middle class domestic living. America turned in upon itself, fed-up with involvement in foreign entanglements. After the hardships of the past, the nation just wanted to settle down. People were ready for a fresh start.

The whole world found itself in an unusual place in the 1950s. At the start of the decade, recovery from World War II was still a fact of life for

many around the globe. At the same time, the United States and the Soviet Union had begun what would come to be known as the "Cold War." The explosion of "suburbia" in America, as new housing became a necessity for the Second World War generation as they married and began families, would become a powerful force in the development of the functional "track housing" that was so quickly constructed across the nation. Suburbia would become a new way of life for millions. The design and construction of such homes would create a whole new ethic of domestic architecture.

As America flexed its muscles as a world power, domestically, the nation could devote itself in the 1950s to investing in important infrastructure development, like the network of interstate highways that opened up automobile travel across the country. This would result in the creation of countless motels and gas stations whose signage would redesign the American environment. Roadside architecture in 1950s America would become an important reflection of American society. Marlboro, Burma Shave, Howard Johnson's, and Texeco embellished the American landscape with a new art form, the billboard and neon sign. Diners and motels across the nation sought to advertise a new American luxury—leisure time. The culture of juke boxes, drive-in movies, car hops, and bowling alleys had arrived.

For the first time in a generation, there was a resumption in the construction of commercial architecture in big American cities. In Chicago, for instance, no new commercial skyscraper had been built since the Crash of 1929 and the resulting Depression at the beginning of the 1930s. World War II saw no new construction projects with all materials going into the vital war effort. The 1950s marked a return to normalcy, to life the way people had remembered it almost twenty years before. A burst of economic prosperity brought the critical resumption of urban development around the country. It also marked the return of large scale consumer production. Automobiles were returning to forefront of American life, now being freely available for the first time in many years. And they were designed to dazzle. Sleek, flashy, and sexy, these machines were all fins and taillights and shining chrome. Seduced, America quickly became a nation of drivers. Television was no longer a scientific

oddity and also came into its own in the 1950s, again altering the shape of American popular culture. Product design and artistry would become a hallmark of this decade. The consumer society was being born. After years of doing without, the nation relished its post-war prosperity and celebrated it with the purchase of conveniences designed for more leisured living. Vacuum cleaners, coffeemakers, radios, phonographs, electric mixers, washing machines, stoves, and other appliances created a new hunger for fresh designs and modern industrial artistry.

The atomic age introduced endless new ideas to American culture. Science fiction, flying saucers, and threats of alien invasions went hand-in-hand with the general paranoia of the times. Together with the advent of America's exploration of space, it wasn't long before this celestial influence began to shape a variety of popular consumer products like lamps, furniture, and kitchen utensils. They soon took on a decidedly "modern," edgy design and space-age artistry.

At the same time, German born Architect Ludwig Mies Vander Rohe, working in Chicago, and others of the International School would introduce America to a style of architectural design that would change the way buildings would be designed for the next forty years. Their glass and steel simplicity, with the absence of any ornamentation, would become a natural blending of the pre-World War II European modernism of the Bauhaus School with the Chicago School of architecture's restrained functionalism.

1960s

Care to our coffin adds a nail no doubt;
And ev'ry grin, so merry, draws one out.

Peter Pindar

Fiberglass furniture. Orange. Avocado. Flowered wallpaper. Pre-fabricated. Modular furniture. Mod fashions. Space-age simplicity. Psychedelic colors. Plastic pods. Acrylics. Minimalist. Futuristic. A rejection of past historical styles of design. Ultra modern. Innovations. Bean bag chairs. Beaded room dividers. Stabiles. Mobiles. Macramé. Lava lamps. Bright colors. Candles. Incense. Strong influence of the Scandinavian designed furniture.

The decade of the 1960s demonstrated a passion for youthful expression and a new modernity of style in popular culture. While it developed on both sides of the Atlantic, it found enormous popularity with the invasion of British music, bands, fashions, and attitude in America. The Beatles, the Rolling Stones, and countless other musical groups imported from Britain became the heralds of a wave of libertine mores and liberal political attitudes. In the United States, the decade began with the election of the youthful John Fitzgerald Kennedy. Within 1,000 days, his assassination would mark a rupture in the optimism of many. The escalation of the American War in Vietnam ignited the forces of political discontent and gave birth to the culture of protest. Over the course of the decade this polarization would become the source of a new voice in artistic expression and mark a rejection of past values and traditions, symbolized in counter cultural lifestyles and tastes. Everything from hairstyles to pants expressed the nuances of political and cultural beliefs. Styles reflecting historically influenced architecture and periods of design were seen as bourgeois and outdated. In America, California was seen to be the epicenter of these new attitudes of the personal freedom, with a culture of more environmentally sensitive living and a heightened spiritual awareness. Flower power was the byword of the new socially conscious and the eyes of many people looked ahead to a liberation of the human person. Old colonies of European powers received independence during this period, which also saw the birth of the civil rights movement in the United States.

The ethereal, environmental bent to the cultural context of this period is best reflected in the proliferation of the use of the flower motif. In addition, the peace symbol became the universal icon of the age. In popular design, items for domestic use reflected high tech simplicity and a

Below: A renewed appreciation for the environment in the 1960s saw a return to nature movement and interest in being close to the earth. This rustic country house is simple and visually at ease in nature. The spacious outdoor deck allows for an even closer connection to nature.

utilitarian sense of aesthetics. Plastic and fiberglass proved inexpensive sources of materials that often could be molded into a variety of domestic forms and uses. On a higher end, modern Danish and Swedish designs in furniture and cabinetry utilizing understated designs in woods like teak, and South American hardwoods, created a popular modernist genre that fit the period's simple tastes. Scandinavian craftsmen were masterful in creating furniture with crisp details in line. Their discreet use of materials fashioned ultra-modern furniture that seemed, at times, to float.

American skylines developed a sleek refinement as new architectural landmarks filled the landscape. Walter Gropius' Pan Am building, was erected in New York in 1963; Skidmore, Owens and Merrill's John Hancock Building rose in Chicago in 1969; and Eero Saarinen fabricated the St. Louis arch in 1963. These remain, today, urban landmarks. The influence of such futuristic styles continue to loom large and retain their integrity.

The 1960s was the decade of space travel too, with tremendous advancements in medicine and science. By the end of the decade America put a man on the moon. The future had arrived and already was reflected in the modernity of the nation's architecture and its futuristic domestic interiors.

Right: Edward E. Carson's Seattle Space Needle and Buckminster Fuller's geodesic dome, both featured at the 1962 Seattle World's Fair, are emblematic of the futuristic design forms that were prevalent during the 1960s. Though the dome was removed immediately following the close of the fair, the Space Needle has gone on to become the very embodiment of Seattle's cityscape.

Gardens

Ah, yet, e'er I descend to th' grave
May I a small house, and a large garden have!

Abraham Crowley

The formal or informal organic system for the designing and shaping of trees, flowers, herbs, and shrubs. Seats, paths, gazebos, and lawns. Hedges, fountains, and lakes. Pergolas, belvederes, and urns.

Gardens have been an indelible part of the human experience since the very beginning of time—see Genesis—and the abounding fertility found in nature has captured the mind and heart of man ever since. Gardens have produced beauty to nourish the aesthetic senses and cultivated edible foodstuffs to nourish the flesh. For some, gardens are private places of solitude and reflection where nature surrounds and uplifts. For others, they are public settings of pastoral grace in which nature envelopes and enriches. Whatever the experience, throughout the centuries gardens have undergone a variety of different stylistic variances when it comes to how to plan and plant them, or how to engage nature in the process of fashioning a garden that expresses a particular aesthetic choice. The world of gardens basically is best seen from the styles that demonstrate their individual approaches. Three basic styles somewhat conveniently describe how gardens have developed over time and how they continue to influence tastes in the present.

The French style is a very formal, artistic, and structured undertaking. Beneath its luxurious traditions of labored gardening, ornamental trees or shrubs are clipped or trimmed into planned shapes or designs called topiaries and ornamental paths are frequently cut between beds of flora, called parterres. True French gardens are very linear and geometric. Often this is reflected in the heavily clipped hedges that frame them. In this tradition, it is as if nature is being systematically controlled by man.

In the English tradition, just the opposite appears true. Everything is made to look as if nature is freely unfolding. It is a more romantic expression of nature where the pastoral is idealized. It is just as labor intensive as the French style, but because everything looks so natural it does not appears to be so formal. This is a luxuriously overgrown look of naturalness and no one added more grace and technique to the English traditional than Capability Brown, the garden architect who reinvented the English style in the mid 18th century. The writer Vita Sackville-West and her husband, Harold Nicolson, however, in 1930, designed one of the most extraordinary gardens in the English tradition at Sissinghurst Castle in Kent. Even today, it remains lush and ethereal filled with grandeur and graced by a thoroughly English touch.

The Japanese style, or the Zen garden, is the third tradition of significant and lasting global prominence. Nature itself appears harnessed in this genre. Known by its austere and manipulated stylings demonstrated in its signature "Bonsai trees," a process of miniaturizing growth through excessive clipping and pruning, it is an ancient and graceful cultural expression. With landscapes

raked and manicured through consistent horticultural maneuvering, this style of small-scale gardening has a deeply spiritual dimension. Its roots, in the contours and traditions of the mysterious East, are brimming with the uncluttered and passionate flavors of an Asian perception of nature and man's role within it. Its artistic minimalism gives it qualities that make it very modern or even futuristic in its simplicity of design. Therefore it lends itself very well to the architectural traditions of modernism. It is often a frequent complementing accompaniment to such understated urban style in both commercial and domestic use.

Among the more extravagant gardens in the English tradition is Chatsworth, the Derbyshire home of the Dukes of Devonshire. The extensive gardens there actually demonstrate four periods of garden design. George London created a formal garden there in the 17th century. It was laid out with canals, an orangery, and fountains. In the 18th century Capability Brown laid out vast parklands and created a wooded park. In the 19th century Joseph Paxton constructed conservatories or glasshouses for cultivating tropical and hard to grow plantings. He fashioned a rookery and added rare conifers. Finally in the 20th century a rose garden was laid out and an herbaceous border was planted. This extraordinary garden is expressive of the long tradition of English garden grandeur.

Irish gardens have added their own unique style to the mix. Driven by a strong delight in the wildness of nature, Irish gardens have traditionally placed little stress on formalism. In the 19th century, William Robinson successfully advocated the idea of building up garden beds, but in such a manner that nature is permitted soon to easily take over with a characteristic wildness. Little symmetry shapes traditional Irish garden design and there is an expressive undercurrent of lush exuberance. Today, Jim Reynolds, Ireland's premier garden architect, continues shaping new gardens of significance and quality in the sub-tropical and extravagant Irish terrain.

Perhaps no one in America has reinvented gardening in popular culture with such passion and salesmanship as Martha Stewart. Her lifestyle formatted television programs and magazine publication have introduced a very up-market interest in domestic gardening. In point of fact, what she has done, almost single handedly, is to introduce American audiences to the realities and the aesthetics of English gardening. She has taught Americans both the vocabulary and the technique of successful gardening. It is a good thing.

Gardens carry out a dramatic aesthetic in permitting man to engage nature and be transformed by its sensuous earthy reality. A hands-on familiarity with gardens and gardening is not difficult. Few have the need today of landscaping by the ethereal Capability Brown. But the work and know-how of all the traditions of gardening are an intimate part of our contemporary living. The transforming power of gardens and gardening deepens the soul and spirit of man.

PART TWO
Architectural Salvage and Today's Homes

How do you shape an interior of inventive elegance or understated grace? What do you need to create a style you can call your own? What will help you fill the rooms of your home with both warmth and interest? Where can you go for innovative and textured ideas of design and décor? What do you need to know to become the architect of your own perfect space? Fashioning such interiors can appear a daunting and complicated task. But that need not necessarily be the case. The threads of taste, fashion, and effective design wind across all the components of everyday living and draw them into aesthetically pleasing combinations. The use of reclaimed architecture in today's homes has significantly enlarged the opportunity to create interiors that are both distinguished and elegant. Decorating needs are enhanced by the availability of architectural elements

A wide selection of unusual artifacts that express timeless beauty and past grandeur are far more readily available today for home use than ever before. In many cities, the careful selection and warehousing of such elements in salvage centers provides a significant resource for creating a perfect interior. Architectural salvage is the harvesting of items from homes or commercial buildings that were often designed with great craftsmanship or architectural excellence. The value of such reclaimed architecture is now more widely appreciated.

What is achievable? You can blend a wide variety of period styles and fashion a distinctive array of various architectural elements to create a refined sense of modern eclecticism. The application of new and alternative uses for salvage elements can make for stunning interiors. You can create as you go, layering your environment with complementary and contrasting textures, as well as conflicting but distinctive periods of architecture. For example, in the midst of shaping an interior in the modern style of the 1960s, the inclusion of a piece of Gothic Revival design can produce highly dramatic effects. The rule here is that there are no rules. Create a new style, highly personal and expressive of your tastes. Broadening your working knowledge of the endless variety of objects that are available should permit you to reshape your domestic landscape and enliven your ability to use and mix the treasures of the past in the interiors of the present.

Discover for yourself what can be found. Learn as you go. Take notes. A hands-on approach will help you shape a discerning attitude that is grounded in the realities of the market place today. You can learn to become adept and articulate about reclaimed architecture. Such knowledge will definitely assist in developing an eye for bargains and a vocabulary to help you ask for what you want. You will also come to know the difference between what has value and artistic merit, and what is simply to be left alone. This should make it easier to answer questions like—"Where is the best resource for period fireplace mantels?" "Where can I locate the best French doors?" and "Should the rusted worn finish on a particular piece of metal be refinished, or left as it is?"

Above: Carved limestone bull's head, circa 1890, from the Detroit Eastern Market, home of the Motor City's wholesale meat industry.

Right: This 65' x 27' living room with 30' ceiling was once a Chicago trucking garage, circa 1920s. The renewed interior features the rustic wooden truss structure and retractable skylights both original to the building. The antique urn filled with French silk pillows, the nickel staircase, and the four nickel lamps add a touch of the Art Nouveau, while the staircase signage adds a decidedly modern touch to the room. It is pure eclecticism.

Columns and Pedestals

Where'er we tred [the coliseum] 'tis haunted, holy ground.

George Gordon, Lord Byron

No element of architecture is more an expression of the grandeur and spectacle of antiquity than the column. It is the very soul of the ancient past. For the ancient Greeks and Romans, columns served a critical function in building design, especially in temples and palaces—they held up the ceiling. Of course, with detailed refinements and arithmetical precision they were also endowed with an extraordinary beauty, carrying the flavor and dramatic spirit of history in their sleek tapering shapes. Three styles of columns are Greek in origin and have their beginnings in the evolving tastes of the fashions of that noble time. We know them by their Greek names—Doric, Ionic, and Corinthian. Two further styles are Roman in origin—Tuscan and Composite.

A whole architectural vocabulary flows from the styles and designs of these five classical varieties of columns. You do not need to be an architect to have a practical familiarity with these various shapes and designs. Taking a little time to learn the key differences among them will give you a sturdy working knowledge of classical tastes. Keep in mind the three essential building blocks of every column—the base, the shaft, and the capital (the top). With some attention to how they are shaped and ornamented, recognizing the various styles will become quite manageable.

Right: In this tableau, a pair of 19th century English cast iron columns stand beside 18th century French louver wooden shutters, an iron vault grate is on the right; in front sits a French wooden garden bench, circa 1900, its present distressed patina is a mark of its elegance. Behind, are a pair of terra cotta shell finials, and on the left a decorative wooden bracket from historic 19th century New Orleans completes the scene.

Below: Detail of a pair of cast concrete columns from the Spanish Revival swimming pool, circa 1940s, of Marshall Field III.

Doric columns are the most simple and the plainest of the three Greek styles. Doric columns have no base. They stand flush with the floor. Their capitals are virtually undecorated round discs of stone. Their shafts have indented ridges and have a slight taper. This style was made famous by its use in the Parthenon—Pericles' monument to the goddess Athena on the Acropolis in Athens.

Ionic columns have very noticeably defined layers that form their base, usually narrow circular bands of stonework. Their capitals have two very distinguished curling scrolls (called volutes) that resemble cinnamon buns or ears. Their shafts, the longest and most tapered, have indented ridges.

Corinthian columns are easy to spot because they are very ornate. Their bases are very well defined circular bands not unlike the Doric. But the heavily encrusted capitals are thick with curling acanthus leaves that give a very three-dimensional sense to its decorations. Their shafts are usually quite slender and ridged.

Tuscan columns (adapted from the Doric) are the very plainest with no decorative designs at all. Their bases are simple rings. Their capitals are

unadorned rounded bands, narrow and plain. Their shafts are thicker at the lower end than at the top and are very smooth without and ridges.

Composite columns are the most embellished of all column styles. They incorporate multiple elements from the other column styles. For instance, their bases are influenced by the multiple rings of the Corinthian. Their tapered shafts are very Ionic with similar ridges. Their capitals exude a very Corinthian motif, thick with acanthus leaves. Their stylized volutes (curling spirals) have Ionic overtones.

Pay attention to the shapes and ornamentation of a column's base, shaft, and capital. It will make the identification of classical columns far less complicated. Perfecting your ability is simple if you live in a reasonably large city as many examples of these styles (or orders as they are more formally known) are a plentiful feature of everyday urban life. Countless government buildings, banks (especially federal), museums, churches, universities, and cemetery monuments in our own times have relied on the beauty and symmetry of classical columns to add dignity, strength, and an air of stability to their external designs. For instance, Chicago's City Hall, a massive building that is a full city block square in size was designed in 1910 with heavy Neo-classical architectural features. Among its central elements are thirty-eight limestone Corinthian columns that frame all four sides of the building. They stretch from the fourth to the ninth floors, giving the appearance they are holding up the great roof. In reality they are purely decorative. But their size, proportion, and ornament add a powerful external drama to the cityscape around it. There is no mistaking the grandeur they add to the purpose or function of this institution.

Columns became a staple of the ancient world of Greece and Rome. A revival of their artistry in contemporary construction during the Italian Renaissance made them very popular again in the refined tastes of the 16th century. When the styles of Greece and Rome were rediscovered and popularized in 18th century England and France, classical columns made a powerful impact on popular tastes and on the future of architecture and decorative design.

Right: This lovely down cushioned settee in a Parisian pied-a-terre carries a distinctive classical style in the small columns that serve as legs. Their tapered elegance serves as a motif to connect this piece of furniture to a timeless refinement. In the niche above the table, two fragments from a Corinthian column add a touch of Greek antiquity to the interior.

Above: The skyline of Chicago's River North neighborhood rises above this unique urban roof garden. Classical composite terra cotta columns were rescued from the McCarthy Building, a late 19th century Chicago skyscraper, and add a special flavor of the immediate past and the classical past. The columns and others terra cotta elements are a splendid frame for the cityscape that rises above this special house designed in the modern style.

Left: The capital from a stylized column fits well into the landscape of this well tended urban garden. It serves as a plant holder, a table for garden parties, and a rich artistic element in its own right. The carved stone element is framed by two black lacquer iron garden chairs.

Left: This column now in use in a lush urban garden was once used in the stone entrance of a 19th century Chicago mansion. Now this highly stylized capital and well polished marble shaft rest in early spring beneath a box of plantings. By summer's end they will spill out of the box and trail down the column.

Stairs and Railings

At the first turning of the second stair
I turned and saw below
The same shape twisted on the banister.

T.S. Eliot

Above: Detail of classic American Victorian balustrade, circa 1880s, displaying the remarkable machine made spindles that were the rage of the age thanks to industrialization. Such manufactured products were dependable, affordable, and responsible for increasing the high quality of interior style.

Right: Stair rail and newel post of inlaid birds-eye maple. The introduction of items of such remarkable quality owed much to the industrialization of the times. Factory made materials permitted a much higher level of artistic design to be incorporated into regular urban dwellings.

Below: A set of early 19th century French oak library stairs with oak rails. This elegant staircase represents a growing 19th century American passion for domestic libraries and their inclusion in the construction of houses of substance and style. The excellence in workmanship and quality of material make this a piece that is easily transferable to other environments and uses.

Oranmore Castle in County Galway is a labyrinth of narrow passageways and stone stairs ripe with the flavor of Medieval Ireland. Few of its stairs are level. You walk slowly, treading in the sloped footsteps of others from the past. Each stair is worn smooth by the footsteps of overlapping centuries. The stairs' primitive composition and the elementary arrangement of materials, however, are very similar to stairs in our own day.

The same can be said for the extravagant stairway in the London home of old Lord Howard de Walden, formerly located near the Ritz Hotel off Green Park in the pre World War I years of the last century. High society, government leaders, and a few royals made grand entrances on these stairs, each formed from rather impressive sheets of lapis lazuli taken from a mine once owned by the old baron. Though the materials of the staircase reached an almost unheard of level of opulence, like that of Kubla Kahn in Zanadu, even these stairs demonstrated a basic utility in their function and design.

Every set of stairs follows a simple formula and design. Three basic components form every stair, from the most elaborate grand marble staircase to the simplest of humble wood. On every stair there is the tread, the horizontal flat surface upon which we step. Then there is the nosing, a kind of overlapping rim or lip. And finally there is the riser, the vertical section by the tip of your shoe, which lifts each step to a higher level.

Railings too are an intricate part of both the practicality of the stairway and its architectural design. While they steady one's balance walking up and down the stairs and prevent the possibility of falling over the stairway's open end, they also offer endless opportunities for high ornamentation and decorative design. The basic components that form a railing are deeply utilitarian in purpose. Each railing, or balustrade, is technically formed from balusters, the individual vertical posts or bars that are held together by the handrail. At the bottom of the stairs and at the upper landing, the rail is held secure by a newel, a large vertical post or beam. Newels also strengthen the diagonal support under the stairs known as the string. When the balusters are attached directly into the stairs themselves, the stairway is referred to as an open string stairway. If the balusters are affixed to the string itself, the stairway is called a closed string stairway. Each style enjoyed periods of popularity. The larger the staircase, the more opportunity for added newels and balusters at further landings. Each of these components lends itself well to designs reflective of the various popular architectural styles of the day.

Before the coming of the age of industrialization, staircases were strictly a handcrafted high-ticket item. They had to be laboriously cut from stone or wood, or fashioned from iron. It was

the method of support within the staircase—these are supported on only one end, permitting them to curve and arch in a most delicate and graceful manner. They were popular in American homes during the Federal period.

When cast iron arrived in the late Georgian period, it was quickly appropriated by staircase makers. It proved to be a reliable and durable material, and it was easy to cast balustrades with highly classical ornamentation. Particularly popular were motifs such as classical roping, wreaths, acanthus leaves, and urns, all portraying the imperial designs of Greco-Roman antiquity. A refined gracefulness was affected in the tapering shape of these fresh, iron handrails and balusters.

Cast iron products flourished throughout the Victorian age, but at the same time, industrialization also influenced the production of wood products

an expensive process requiring a large expenditure of family capital. The hand wrought staircase was a serious investment in a large house and, quite literally, it was a reflection of the importance of house and the wealth of the family who had it built. Architects took great pride in fashioning staircases that displayed their abilities. In the 18th century, the balusters and the newel posts of stairways were appealing elements to ornament in the Neo-classical style. For instance, newel posts were frequently designed in the shape of a classical column, while others were adorned with finials in the shape of classical spheres or urns. Balusters, still turned and carved by hand, were commonly affixed directly into the treads (this was the age of the open string), with two or three handsome balusters per stair. At times, a variety of styles were mixed throughout the balusters. Because of the popularity of the open string stairway, the stair ends were able to receive rich classical embellishment and continued the motif of the overall design. Rich woods, highly polished, were used in the fashioning of the rails and added a dramatic refinement.

The cantilevered staircase was a highly popular style in homes of prominence in the early decades of the 19th century. Cantilevering denotes

and saw the advancement of methods and techniques that simplified the process of wooden stairway construction. The introduction of new machinery for cutting and trimming now made the elaborate design styles of the past more affordable and highly styled products began to appear in ordinary houses—good stairways were becoming a staple part of home interior design. Soon, elaborate newel posts and well-carved balusters grew to be an important feature of new middle-class Victorian homes.

The influence of the Arts and Crafts movement heightened interest in having items of quality in the home. Well-crafted stairways provided an important focal point for the addition of finely designed wood rails and handsomely carved wood balusters. Arts and Crafts revised many styles from the historic past, such as the 16th or 17th century. Fashioning simple but evocative staircases, the movement captured popular tastes with its poetic artistry and its influence revitalized the framed newel staircase that featured a solid plank constructed balustrade of hardwoods such as oak. Both the design and the rich wood planking produced a warm, panel-like effect that went far beyond the utility of the stairway. It was the beauty of

Left: An American Victorian walnut newel post, balustrade, and finial, circa 1880. The intricate craftsmanship so luxuriously displayed here would have been difficult and prohibitively expensive for ordinary middle class individuals before the advent of industrialization. Burnham, the progenitor of outstanding Chicago School architecture, displays his high ability for domestic design in this staircase.

Right: A classic American Victorian 19th century balustrade and curving handrail, reflecting the passion in the period for machine made spindles. The rise in the use of machine made products made such finely designed elements of style affordable in many homes. The handcrafting of such a sculptured rail would have been very costly.

the highly polished wood itself, rather than any ornate embellishment, that became the key decorative feature of Arts and Craft design. Though its origins are in the second half of the 19th century, its appealing unadorned simplicity would remain a standard of stairway design throughout the 20th century. In America, architect Howard Van Doran Shaw enhanced this rustic tradition, creating some of America's most refined Arts and Craft mansions.

The Gothic Revival movement, of the mid 1850s and beyond, also produced remarkably rich staircases thick with romantic medieval embellishment and appeal. Newel posts rose on stairways like cathedral spires, encrusted with castellated fretwork and charm. Elegant carved tracery, trefoil, and quatrefoil balustrades, along with Gothic arcading, replicated the regal fantasy world of the Middle Ages. Foliated crockets, chevron molding, castellated carvings, and fluting attempted to recreate the magic time when knighthood was in flower. And public tastes found this style intriguing—it became fashionable and an important expression of the interest and vogue in things medieval, like Sir Walter Scott's heroic literary tales of chivalry and honor, such as Ivanhoe.

It is a curious feature of stairways that their individual components—treads, risers and nosing, railings, balustrades, individual balusters, and newel posts—are often more salvageable and of more practical value than the whole stairway itself. Perhaps it is their relationship to the design of the particular house for which they were constructed that makes the reuse of an entire stairway difficult. It is a little like a boat in the basement. However, stairways can be salvaged in their entirety. Most frequently they are acquired through teardowns and if they are of sufficient value, they might be saved for reuse. Many years ago, William Randolph Hearst purchased the grand bifurcated oak staircase from Eyrecourt Castle, an elaborate 17th century Irish country house in County Galway. The stairway was packed up and boxed more than half a century ago. Today, it remains crated in the storage vaults of the Detroit Institute of Art. It would take a very special house to contain such an extraordinary set of stairs today.

The reuse and installation of a full stairway retrieved from any house can be a daunting task. It works best when a new house or restoration project can incorporate a stairway in the early stages of construction by building around it. There was a very controversial incident several years ago when the

Left: A sweeping chrome Art Deco seahorse-themed staircase with stone steps winds its way from a Neo-classical door surround with broken pediment presenting a remarkable contrast of design periods.

Right: This rich carved oak staircase with oak newel posts in the Arts and Crafts style adds a high elegance to the interior of a Lake Forest mansion.

Below: This black lacquered wrought iron staircase is both an entrance to and an extension of an urban garden by its lush arrangement of flowers and plants on each step. By summer's end, the stairway will be thick with growing things.

Arts Club of Chicago was required to vacate their premises. The former site of the club was scheduled for demolition. Many years before, the great modern architect Ludwig Mies Van der Rohe had designed the club's main stairway. It was a minimalist metal staircase of considerable historic merit and became the cause celebre in attempts to save the building. When all options were gone, the club built a new structure and had the Mies staircase installed in their new home. The stairway made an easy adaptation, for the building was built around it.

Stairways that are not used as an entire structure or whole can provide an endless stream of imaginative and practical applications for use of its parts. One of the very best is in the fabrication of a rood screen, a popular device in medieval ecclesiastical architecture that provides a stylized grillwork to mask the open area behind an altar. In a rectangular frame divided into thirds by flat horizontal beams, the turned balusters, or carved staircase spindles, are arranged along a section fitted between the beams above and below. With a tapestry or piece of heavy fabric hung behind the screen, the spindles make an architecturally significant addition to any room.

Sections of a balustrade, particularly an iron balustrade, can be use effectively in bathrooms as a towel holder. They can also be used to form radiator covers, shelving, and book cases.

Newel posts have the widest adaptive use of any stairway component, as they frequently can be reset into other stairway rails efficiently and effectively. Newels of particular craftsmanship and period architectural design acquire an artistic value unattached from the stairway. They are substantial elements by themselves and can make a significant contribution to the beauty of any room. If there are a pair or series of pairs of newels, they can be use as unifying decorative ornaments in a large room like a loft. Finials also transfer well from one stairway to another. But finials themselves can have multi-uses as elements of ornamental design. Stairways offer a rich and fertile harvest of architectural elements.

Doors and Door Fittings

"Is there anybody there?" said the traveler, knocking on the moonlit door.

Walter de la Mere

No element of architectural design has had more practical significance for the home or more evolving aesthetic influence than the door. They can be strictly utilitarian—a barrier to the outside. Or they can be the very heart of high elegance—refined, detailed, enchantingly inviting—a welcome to all to pass. But whether they swing, slide, or slam, doors are an indelible part of any home. They provide a wide sweep of necessary human need—privacy and security, protection and seclusion, room to breathe, or a way to escape. Left open, doors transmit a willingness to engage others. Close and barred, doors shut out the annoying, intrusive, and unrelenting sight and sounds of the world, including the weather. Sometimes this was achieved with more deliberate style and grace.

Doors occupied a strategic significance in more violent and aggressive tribal and feudal times. From the Middle Ages to the Renaissance their construction and form were heavy duty. Guarding the door was a matter of some well-founded concern. Doors were essential for the safety of the house, its inhabitants, and their possessions. Usually they were constructed with more attention to strength than beauty. Heavy timbers, joined by crossed planks, were fastened into place with iron fittings for hinges and latches. Doors had little if any embellishment except for the handcrafted ironwork that included a rudimentary iron device with which the door was barred. The ring handles, drop handles, and iron pulls were popular types of wrought iron fittings and a great luxury. Doors were often reinforced with iron nails, while hinges were extended across the door planks to provide added reinforcement and strength.

While entry doors received artistic embellishment during the Baroque period of the 17th century, it was during the revivalist expression of Neo-classicism in the 18th century that the door received its most expansive and formal refining. For architects of the period, the main entry door became the key feature of the Georgian façade. In executing the designs of the great Italian architect Andrea Palladio, the entry way became part of a larger series of intricate complementary adornments. For instance, the familiar influence of ancient temple design—columns, pediments, corbels, and carved hoods framed the entrance area and surrounded the door with architectural proportion and linear ornamentation that became a principal feature of design. With the inclusion of a glass transom called a fanlight, outside light was able to fill the interior entrance halls of houses. Its prominent position above the door completed the symmetry of the Georgian entryway's overall formal design.

The doors around which all this grandeur was set were bold and elegant. Double rows of wooden panels accentuated the door's understated linear design and added a geometric ornamental texture. The development of new intricate mechanical lock systems, added to the fresh modernity of the door. This hardware was displayed with great beauty and frequently was fashioned from

Left: A pair of late 18th century oak timber French doors. Their size, ten feet in length, gives a handsome sense of proportion. The original iron hinges are hand hammered and the panels are battened by metal studs original to the door. The rough-hewed patina gives a sturdy, fortress-like feel. Some carving atop the center molding adds an elegance and high craftsman-like finish.

Right: Hand wrought iron door hinges in medieval motif from a large Gothic Revival door.

to the tastes of those seeking a return to a more unadorned expression of craftsmanship. Their farmhouse-like character indulged the movement in its quest for quality over quantity in the age of mass production.

The paneled door, however, proved to be a more popular and agile style for interiors from the early 18th century onward. Its basic construction design includes a vertical wooden frame with slotted grooves into which rectangular panels are tightly fitted. Little change has been made in this design over the years. Variations in the numbers of panels and the artistic details of the beveling around the panels are the only real alteration over the past 300 years. Paneled doors required far less intense labor in the construction process than battened plank doors, and far less solid

highly polished brass. Brass doorknobs further accentuated the elegance of the ornamentation, together with a brass mail slot. Doors were highly lacquered and painted a deep rich dark color. The luster of their shiny patinas came from the dozens of coats of lacquer required to keep a door in its gleaming stately condition.

wood in their fabrication. The advancements made in the techniques of cutting and in assembling materials added a further economic advantage to paneled doors.

In America, classical surrounds grew popular and flourished because of the access to pattern books that aided in detailing the most refined of designs. Most surrounds in America were fashioned of available woods rather than stone. But the grandest entry doors were found on the plantations of the Deep South fashioned in the Greek Revival style. Their wide wraparound porches were a practical extension of the classical façade and evolution in design to accommodate life in the warm climate of the region. Fanlights and porticoes, towering columns, and grand doorways accentuated the social nature of the antebellum plantation porch.

Paneled doors easily projected the linear symmetrical proportions expressed in Neo-classical architectural design and were a unifying theme when used throughout a house. In the later 18th century, a growing artistry in the framework surrounding interior doors added further refinements of Neo-classical style. For instance, the addition of a carved pediment, either whole or broken, above a door and the further application of classical motifs such as acanthus leaves, flowers, urns and swags, and scrolled pediments expanded the size of interior doors and their architectural influence. Doors with six panels were the standard style. During this period double doors also became fashionable in reception rooms and drawing rooms. The ability to open both simultaneously afforded both host and hostess a grandeur to entrances and exits. Most doors of the period are made from hardwoods such as mahogany, rosewood, and oak in better houses. They were heavily waxed and varnished. Pine and cheaper grades of fir and other softwoods were utilized in lesser interiors and often painted.

Interior doors have been a significant part of domestic design since the Middle Ages. Their function has been more a matter of internal privacy than protective security. As a result they have received and expressed a wide array of ornamental and decorative embellishment that incorporated them into a larger interior design theme. The basic form of interior doors has undergone little evolution over the periods. Plank doors that today reflect a rustic rural simplicity were very prevalent as interior doors up to the 17th century and have enjoyed revival periods of popularity in other eras of architectural fashion. During the Arts and Crafts movement of the mid 19th century, for instance, their more rudimentary style was highly appealing

In Victorian times, doors with four panels become fashionable, and later in the century two panels become the standard style. Glass panels also

Above: Late 19th century French chateau door, with distressed wood patina and wrought iron and glass panels. The excellence of this ironwork, and the opaque glass panel behind it, has great utility as well as beauty. The curving style of the ironwork has a decidedly French Nouveau style and provides an added measure of domestic security. The glass adds a layer of privacy while still permitting light to filter through it. History and elegance live still in these doors.

Above right: This pair of early 20th century French bakery doors have rich amber and gold art glass with leading and a figurative emblem of the bakery guild further executed in colored glass. This glass permits easy visibility in a busy bakery setting and at the same time injects a refined elegance by the craftsmanship and materials used.

Right: This pair of Belgian Art Deco glass doors is emblematic of this refined avant-garde movement. The geometric design of the art glass displays the restraint and linear fashion so common to the Art Deco style. These doors carry a historic provenance in their Belgian origins, as it is believed that the Art Deco movement began there.

Left: Late-19th century American Art Nouveau doors with amber and mauve stained glass panels. Such doors were enormously popular and represented the very latest fashion with a decidedly French touch. The popular use of art glass in this period permitted light to scatter the familiar darkness of Victorian domestic interiors.

Below: Scottish Art Nouveau wooden door with art glass panel. The fluid floral design within the glass displaying a bending tulip at the top is typical of the heavily organic style. The Scottish origins of this particular door are a decidedly eminent pedigree, as Scottish Deco artists created some of the world's finest.

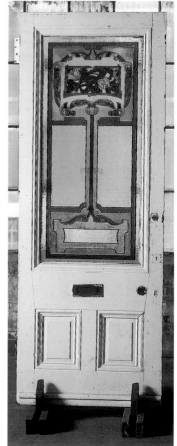

Left: This appears to be more of a door system than a door. But these mid-19th century American Greek Revival interior doors and entry arch display the understated refined symmetry of this very popular American architectural style. Originally these doors were set in one of America's most prestigious Revival homes, an Ohio River Valley house in Madison, Indiana.

Right: American Art Modern bronze eight foot elevator doors from the 1940s–1950s. This style expresses a sturdy utilitarian modernity while stressing a simplicity in embellishment. This was a popular style used with great success in high-ticket American commercial high-rise properties. The style connotes a sleek, almost Art Deco restraint emphasizing rather than disguising the purpose and function for which these doors were made.

began to be added into paneled doors, permitting an infusion of natural light into the relatively dark interiors of the periods. Such glass was often etched, adding privacy to a room. The use of stained glass and colored glass also became a popular Victorian affectation. The process of making paneled doors became fully automated during this industrial age. Sliding doors that recessed into pocketed wall space became very popular in America in the grandest homes: in addition to their highly polished wood grained panels, these doors permitted lengthy expansion of interior rooms. With the pocket doors open rooms flowed into one another accommodating social functions and large gatherings of people.

Doors have continued to offer wide opportunity for artistic expression in further developments in architectural design. The organic fluidity of the Art Nouveau movement's style used etched glass and colored art glass in both exterior and interior door design. The Art Deco style of metal and glass proved to have an effective application in door design. Art Deco doors were simple and highly modern, and became a focal point of interior artistry.

The popularity of plywood doors from the 1930s on altered the shape and quality of many interior domestic doors. Because the use of veneer bonded panels of inexpensive composite woods, door panels began to disappear in common use. Metal frame wire glass doors also appeared.

The most substantial development in the technology and mechanics of door fabrication came in the evolution of stronger, more dependable, and more affordable hardware and fittings. These ranged from very elementary plank door accessories wrought from iron, such as strap hinges and handles, thumb-latch locks, and lock box mechanisms, to the elegant high rubbed finishes of brass door plates, lever handles, push plates, and decorative keyhole escutcheons of the 18th century. From the brass rim locks and cast iron key holes of the 19th century, to the tumblers and dead bolts of modern times, door hardware has fashioned ever more practical methods of protection, while maintaining an elegant artistry of quality details.

Door hardware—knobs, lock plates, hinges, kick plates, and handles are highly sought after elements of architectural design. Most salvage centers have good supplies of vintage hardware materials and it is usually possible to find items such as hand-wrought iron hinges or handles or pull rings, though you might have to really search them out. Brass fittings are popular items too. Some homeowners might be looking for a very particular style of knob. They might require six brass knobs or eight porcelain knobs. These can be found, but, again, it may very well take some added effort to find a set of similar pieces. Supplies vary from place to place, and so does the quality.

Searching out hardware can be more difficult than sorting through larger and more expensive architectural items, but beauty is in the details and it can often be worth a patient search. Vintage brass items are particularly good buys. They may look discolored when you find them in the salvage yard, but they will shine up to a high gloss easily. Well-crafted brass door fittings are timeless and beautiful ornamental elements.

The most sought after doors in salvage centers are varnished doors. They are high on everyone's list for they can be easily stripped, sanded, and re-stained. Whether its hard wood or soft, salvage sellers say the varnished move the quickest.

Hardwoods are the most durable of doors for reuse. If you want strength, then look for mahogany, rosewood (rare), oak, cherry, or birch, though you might want to consider any other woods that you might have around the home and match oak with oak for example. Some buyers are in the market for a unique wood, like heart pine that is quarter-sawed. This unique method of cutting, provides a luxurious finish to the wood, a sensuous texture that comes from the sawing technique. It is an

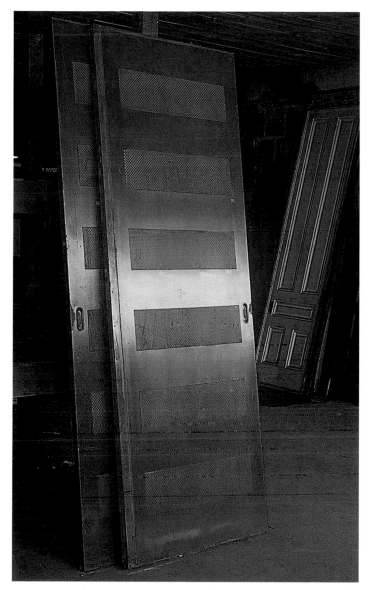

expensive and a wasteful method, but the final product is outstanding. Another specialty item are doors with surrounds. Doors of unusually high quality often come with the entire panel that frames the door—the jamb, and perhaps a highly ornamental pediment. Such decorative surrounds can be found in many Greek Revival interiors. They are, of course, rarer, but can make a really wonderful addition to a home.

When building a new home or rehabilitating an old one, doors reclaimed from salvage offer endless opportunities for shaping interiors of character and beauty. Vintage doors are not difficult to discover. What might be difficult is six or eight all exactly the same. One method of circumventing this problem is to use high quality doors each having a very different style. Make sure you know the measurements of your doors when you go out to look.

As well as their traditional use, doors can be put to service in a number of other ways. For instance, a door of fine quality wood can be used along a wall horizontally as a type of wainscoting. Turned on their sides, doors of fashionable woods, such as rosewood, oak, and poplar, add a real distinction in this way.

Doors also can be used as the headboard of a bed, where those with highly ornamental design or tooled crafting can look spectacular. Horizontally, they can also be easily fitted to the side frames of a bed. Vertically, their height can add a very dramatic shape and texture to both bed and bedroom.

Doors make good bars too, either with the addition of four legs, or by fitting the door across a cabinet. Perhaps it could be a door that holds some special significance like the door to your old house. Perhaps the door itself has its own special grandeur such as the door from a church or cathedral.

Hinged together three or four doors can be fashioned into a screen for use as a small accent piece in a large room or a way to section off a very large space as in a loft.

French doors always bring a touch of elegance and they are not just limited to use within a home's interior. Setting the French doors out in the garden in a frame is an unusual way to show off their beauty.

If you find a good panel door, place sheets of mirrors in the panels. Set the door against a wall, adding sparkle to the room.

Art glass doors can be hung horizontally from the ceiling and back lit. The beauty of the glass will shine and create a wonderful canopy in a special room.

The best use for a door though, is that for which it was intended, and remember, the main door of any house is a focal point for viewing its overall structure and design. Find a door with character and pedigree. It is probably the first thing anyone will notice.

Windows and Shutters

With antique pillars massy proof,
And storied windows richly dight,
Casting a dim religious light.
Let the pealing organ blow,
To the full-voiced quire below.

John Milton

Above: Detail from late-19th century American stained glass funereal window once used in a family mausoleum.

Right: The pine shutters in this circa 1873 Italianate row house continue to provide textured utility, complementing the linear form of the crown molding and window surrounds. Without any textile draperies, the shutters permit privacy and the ability to darken the room. The maneuverable louvers allow for control over both airflow and light. Brass fittings, industrially made, add a layer of elegance.

Below: Framed leaded stained glass window showing a portrait of Shakespeare rich in intricate detail and easily adaptable for domestic use.

Windows and shutters have a remarkable utilitarian immediacy about them. Their function and purpose are instantaneous—fresh air and sunlight. These two most necessary natural elements are central to architecture and have have governed the size and shape and design of windows and shutters from the earliest of days. They are a passage to the outside world, a connection to nature, and a protective barrier against its forces.

The form of windows has been a long-evolving feature of architectural design. The most significant determinant in that development was the availability of glass. Though glass as a substance has been used for three millennia, as a fragile and rare commodity it has a relatively short history in domestic architecture. Long before glass could be fabricated in any abundance, wood, oiled paper, and skins were frequently used as a way to keep the elements out from domestic interiors. Window openings were small to minimize heat loss, though this, of course, restricted the availability of natural light and fresh air. Such early windows were primitive and coarse and glass was a scarce and highly prized commodity. When it was available for use in windows, panes were small, thick, and required leading. Only when the expansion of glass-making technologies evolved to produce more dependable forms of glass could any reasonable supply of it allow large-scale domestic window treatments.

The 18th century saw the development of more reliable types of glass. Glass could now be formed into larger pieces for use in windows, thus allowing their shape and form to expand. This essentially led to the development of the sash window, in which glass panes were fitted into separate top and bottom windows that could be lifted and opened from the bottom. A series of wooden pins permitted opened windows to be held in place. Windows, at the time, were placed flush to the outside walls of a building, but in the city of London, a 1709 law governing the construction of buildings held that for issues of public safety, windows would have to recede four inches from any outside wall and sit more deeply into the interior of the façade. This modification led to their accommodation within a window well of sufficient space to hold a mechanism of counter-weights needed to lift sash windows and keep them open without the use of wooden pegs. While it would take another twenty years for these sash windows to become a prevalent feature in most homes, in the process the modern window was born.

With further developments in the process of good glass-making, window treatments of dramatic beauty and architectural excellence flourished in fashionable houses and it became the

custom to accentuate the central window in the design of distinguished houses. The façades of Georgian houses expanded during the century and an extensive embellishment of their windows followed. For instance, during this era Neo-classical decorative ornamentation increased, adding triangular pediments as eyebrows on exterior windows, together with balustrades, engaged columns, and pilasters. Windows added to the proportioned symmetry of gracious house design and provided a variety of window embellishment that was complementary to the overall façade of the house. Upper windows were less elaborate than those on lower floors that tended to receive a full array of classical ornamentation.

During this period shutters were an interior element used to control the flow of air and natural light within an individual room. Designed in such a way as to conveniently fold into the wall

Left: A colorful art glass segmented window is used as a decorative kitchen shelf affixed to distressed wrought iron brackets. The window is high up on the wall and is surprisingly durable, holding vases and a wire cake tier.

Right: Superb Prairie windows from the studio of Frank Lloyd Wright are suspended in a large window-scape of a home designed in the modern style. The light dances through the art glass bevels and becomes a source of added texture in this large room. In the center is a sprite, also designed by Wright, from his Midway Gardens, a once spectacular Chicago dance venue that was torn down in the late 1920s. On the right is a Wright wall sconce.

surrounding a window, they were functional and practical. Early Georgian shutters were solid pieces of wood plank, but later in the century they evolved into the familiar louver style that permitted even more regulation of sunlight and fresh air. Controlling the available level of sunlight was important for the protection of fabric and painting that could easily be damaged by the full force of the sun.

During the mid 19th century there was a high interest in the return of the casement window of the 15th century. Casement windows arose in a period when glass was so precious that it existed in none but the wealthiest homes. Small individual glass panels were leaded into a window that was hinged and latched. It became fashionable during the Arts and Crafts movement to replicate this style in the newer brick homes of the period as a reminder of a time before industrialization when the skills and handiwork of master artisans had higher standards of aesthetic idealism. The Gothic Revival, which spread through England and the United States in the latter decades of the Victorian era, found casement windows a naturally romantic expression of medieval style as there was often a taste of the ecclesiastical in

their shapes and designs, particularly noticable in the inclusion of stained glass in decorative traceries. Casement windows were also attractive and practical, maintaining a place in popular tastes past the turn of the century when adopted by the architects of the Edwardian period.

Growing advances in the technology of glass making created stronger, more durable, and more fashionable glass over the decades of the 20th century. And better glass allowed its more dramatic use as an element of building construction itself. The modern school of architecture came to rely on resilient high-tech glass in modern skyscraper design and it also became a substantial modern element of both design and architectural ornamentation. The extensive use of glass by American architects Mies Van der Rohe and Phillip Johnston, particularly in domestic architecture, established a new harmony between man and nature in their famous glass boxes. Nature becomes stunningly engaged as walls of glass removed visual barriers between interior and exterior life.

Windows and shutters are highly readaptable architectural elements in high demand at reclamation centers and salvage yards. They are

abundantly easy to find and add significant character to any architectural project for the home. Naturally the use of reclaimed windows in any undertaking produces a serious set of construction preconditions. Among the most popular windows from the past periods of design introduced into contemporary settings are windows of Victorian art glass. Stained glass is another window style that makes itself adaptable to modern domestic interiors. Their use in special rooms interjects a dramatic and historic layer of textures and colors. Both these types of windows can be installed into pre-existing domestic window frames, if the dimensions are right. They can also be hung—suspended in front of interior windows providing maximum light. Another method for utilizing a stained glass window is even more dramatic. Suspend the window from the ceiling and back-light it well. This will allow the artistry of the glass to create a more exotic atmosphere.

Windows offer a wide and creative series of fresh possibilities for design and ornamentation. For instance, a window of unusual architectural style, a long panel of French windows, or leaded beveled glass, can be used to highlight a view or panorama by suspending it outside in a garden from a tree, or even better, set off in the distance to frame a view. Large Gothic windows with tapering arched tops would make a grand perspective set off in a field or rolling lawn. On an urban rooftop, the same can be done to frame a cityscape. Several windows of expansive proportion might be secured to create a line of "windows" without walls. They will provide a curious setting for outdoor dinners and soirees. Smaller windows might be used as the doors on medicine cabinets or all your kitchen cabinets. Windows, particularly those with interesting glass, can be hung on the wall to great effect. A dozen small quarter pane windows lined symmetrically around a large room creates a textured interior, particularly in a minimalist space.

If you find a group of matching windows, leaded Welch casement windows for instance, or hand blown green glass windows, use them to create a wall between rooms. It will be a splendid piece of room art, as well as a way to delineate the space in a large open area like an urban loft. Windows could also be lined up, one next to the other to make a fence of glass. Use windows like you would use the panels of a picket fence. If you

Far left: A fresh use of an old eight-paned window is found when it becomes an unusual frame for this primitive American farm painting of a pig. The distressed finish of the window frame is a remarkable complement to the painting and adds a strong "country" feel to the room.

Left: A large stack of circa 1870s Italianate wooden shutters offers a wide variety of uses.

fashion an interesting louvered fence, particularly if they are tall. Shutters can be hinged and utilized as folding screens that can be used on lawns and beaches to create a setting for a dinner or a party. They help in reducing wind yet the louvers still permit controlled airflow. They can really help in keeping linens and table settings from being blown asunder while dining outdoors.

In looking for shutters, search for the ones that have the most distressed finishes. Find the ones that are the most tall and slender. It is a personal matter, but think carefully about disturbing the

find some interesting brackets, you can turn a window (art glass works particularly well) into a shelf in your kitchen, or anywhere for that matter, to hold glassware—windows make the perfect holder for stemmed martini glasses. Long tall windows can also be hinged to make a triptych that can be hung on a wall or placed on a table. Take the glass out of an interesting window frame and put in mirrors and hang them in groups with candles in front of them for unusual lighting.

Shutters also lend themselves to inventive and exciting uses. In a salvage yard, you might come upon a large number of shutters from a house teardown or from the porch of some resort or hotel. They can be used to

personality of their aged look. Crackled paint finishes can be a real find—the shabbier the better. You can, of course, always use shutters in the manner for which they were designed, to control the flow of air and sunlight inside the rooms of your house. Hang shutters larger than your windows and when you close them you will realign the sight lines in the room. Perhaps you will find a very long, 18th or 19th century French shutter that you could hang on the wall and create a tableau around. If used in this way refinishing is particularly unappealing. Let the roughness add its own character to your interior—unleash an artistry that cannot be found in a can of paint.

Mantels and Fireplaces

Farewell rewards and fairies, Good housewives now may say,
But now foul sluts in dairies do fare as well as they,
And though they sweep their hearths no less than maids were wont to do,
Yet who of late for cleanliness, Finds sixpence in her shoe.

Richard Corbet

Above: English mid-Victorian Royal Doulton glazed tile fireplace formerly in a London townhouse with a motif of "putti" roasting chestnuts. The popularity of Royal Doulton's signature china was a high mark of English artistic sensibilities for the Victorians. Owning a fireplace mantel created by their studios would have been a sign of artistic celebrity. An Arts and Crafts touch radiates out of this singular piece.

Right: American Victorian white Cararra marble fireplace mantel with machine made engravings, circa 1870s. Hearths by this period have become smaller as coal became more economical and more available for urban dwellers. The refinements of this piece are easily complemented by the Second Empire gilt mirror, the silver side lamps, 18th century Chinese bowls, and the 19th century American grave finial on the mantel.

Below: Early 19th century English Oak fireplace mantle with rich carved detail.

Fireplaces have always enjoyed a special place in any domestic dwelling. For centuries, they have cast a thoroughly practical and romantic shadow on any room in which they are used. Fireplaces and mantels have always been a visual expression of how art and utility translate into the elements of architectural design—fireplaces have been fashioned for practical necessity, mantels for aesthetic beauty. Together, they blend period elegance with human need. In this process, mantels and fireplaces developed a unique attachment to one another and became an essential component of domestic life.

The fireplace mantel remains the ultimate all-purpose element of reclaimed architectural salvage. It is the most sought after of any piece of historical architectural design and the most functional example of a vintage element's use in a contemporary home. Homeowners who had never ventured out to a salvage center say that they usually did so first in search of a fireplace mantel. There is no bigger draw and mantels are the aortic valve of most architectural salvage centers' life of success. The mantelpiece has a unique ability to find continuous reuse in home design, a measure of which is due to their physical durability. The stone, marble, wood, or cast iron materials most commonly used to make the vintage mantel provided them with a strength that is as significant as their aesthetic beauty. In short, most mantelpieces have been made to last. They are now the most common item to be removed from a house before demolition, and the fact that the fireplace was such a common feature of domestic architecture throughout the past, means that there is an abundant supply of them in the present.

Over the centuries, the fireplace has undergone an evolution that transformed it from the simple, rough utilitarian hearth of cottage and castle, to the refined, ornamented centerpiece of family life. The fireplace once served not only as the essential source of domestic heating, but also as its chief center of cooking and often the single source of interior illumination as well, making it the sustaining component of family life. The interiors of the pre-industrial past, for many, were essentially one large, primitive room in which most aspects of family life unfolded. Fireplaces, as we know them today, only developed their distinctive function when the interiors of dwellings began to be redefined and individual rooms emerged with separate and specific functions of their own. When the kitchen was ultimately separated from the other rooms of the house, it not only changed the way in which people ate, but it reorganized how people lived and socialized with others.

Technological advances in the methods of construction and venting in fireplace design during the early days of the 16th century went a long way to civilize its basic form into something

we would recognize today. No one wanted a room full of smoke, so advances in chimney design and hood construction led to better ventilation and to the implementation of the basic flue that was far more efficient than crudities of the past in the eradication of smoke. This, in turn, unleashed further design changes in the construction of the brick fire wall. The family hearth would never be the same again. The basic shape of the newly evolved hearth provided ample opportunity for ornamentation, chiefly applied to the wood or stone lintel framing its open mouth. In effect, the mantel was born.

As an external design element, the mantel has its origins in the artistic and architectural achievement of the Renaissance. During this era, the addition of a stone or marble frame around the hearth opening was greatly embellished with classical motifs and adorned with further elements of architectural ornament, such as columns and pilasters and intricately carved figures along a frieze. Rising out of this flourish of inventiveness came the mantel that even today, five centuries later, has undergone little change.

However, fireplaces have continued to demonstrate unique artistic and technological refinements over the centuries. As the most central and significant element of architectural design in many homes, they became dramatic and powerful expressions of popular tastes and changing fashions. In many ways, they were symbolic representations not only of period styles, but also of the growing tides of a family's rising fortune. Fireplaces were status symbols in the 18th and 19th centuries in much the same way that fancy cars and swimming pools helped define status for many in the 20th century.

Once you remove the roasting joint of meat on a spit from the fireplace, the hearth becomes a different place. For a start it does not need to be so big. When cauldrons no longer bubble above the embers, and the residue of domestic cuisine is no longer spilling over on the living room floor, a new civility appears and a significant socio-cultural shift is underway. Couple this domestic upward trend with the ever-expanding size of the family purse through successful commercial enterprise, and all the pieces are in place for an important step up the social food chain.

Nothing expressed the brightening fortunes of 18th century Britain more than the large scale passion for architectural design. And no feature of interior elegance better suited the exuberant growth and refined domesticity than did the family hearth. It was a mirror of unfolding family fortunes. This is the century that saw the aggrandize-

ment of the parlor fireplace as the center of family life and as the emblem of family prestige.

Thanks to the plentiful prevalence in the 18th century of architectural pattern books that catalogued and diagrammed the specifics of design and ornamentation, a whole new day dawned in the life of the domestic fireplace. All the aesthetic splendor of classical form and style was made available through these remarkably helpful texts and fireplaces began to assume an important position as the focus of the period's Neo-classical designs. This was reflected in the materials used to fashion mantelpieces of unparalleled elegance.

Marble proved to be the choice material among the wealthiest of homes. Expensive and hard to acquire, strictly from import, it had been a favorite from the time of classical antiquity itself and added a distinctive layer of history to the eminence of any design. It was extravagant, demonstrative, and refined, and thus expressed the character of the commercial barons of the day. Creamy white, statuary marble, from the quarries of Cararra in Italy, was employed for the finest of commissions as it had an extraordinary temperament that permitted it to be carved into the most precise of classical shapes. Other forms of marble were also highly prized and were often used to accentuate the decorative themes. Onyx, black as pitch, rich reds, lush as cinnamon, and variegated deep veined marbles were used in intricate inlays to fashion elaborate fireplace surrounds that echoed the new aesthetic for lavish, grandiose, classical styles. Pediments and friezes, scrolling lintels, and refined Ionic columns were each employed with much attention given to proportion and fine detail. The popular tastes thrived on classical motifs, such as mask and swag carvings or roundels that featured delicate figures from mythology.

Throughout the developments in design and ornamentation, the basic form of the fireplace mantel, or surround, was altered very little. Both the most ornate and the most simple shared a basic structural rectilinear shape of two upright support posts and a beam. In the shifting of popular tastes, these elements might expand and be elaborately embellished and adorned. However, the basic structural form remained intact.

In more modest houses, fireplace surrounds were made of wood, which also took detailed embellishment. Ornate surrounds were executed in exquisitely carved woods that were far more economical due to their ready accessibility. Classical detailing, such as bead molding, acanthus leaves, egg and dart motifs, carved columns, and ribboned urns accentuated the rich surfaces of the wood. By the end of the 18th century, the mantel surround reached new heights as fuller adornment went on to include an intricately tooled area of design that rose high above the mantel shelf. Often this was designed to hold a painting or an elaborate mirror.

By the end of the 18th century, the pendulum of public tastes began to move back to more simple, less ornate classical designs, but the most far reaching change to affect the style and shape of fireplace design came with

Left: Chicago fireplace mantelpiece of blue gray marble, circa 1880s. The machine-carved marble was a wonder of artistry that came with the enhanced machine technology of the period. The narrowed cast iron hearth was designed for burning coal that was both available and cheap. It expresses a domestic coziness that is timeless today.

the growing use of coal as a more efficient fuel. The discovery of coal deposits in England and Wales had a profound influence upon the domestic fireplace. Coal produced a more intense heat, but it required different conditions to maximize its potential and the wide mouthed hearths of the past proved inefficient. Coal required a tighter hearth and a different flow of oxygen than wood and this initiated a reduction in the size of the fireplace. At the same time, the practical solution to this necessity proved to be the reworking of traditional fireplace tools like the firedog and fire grate. Firedogs, or andirons, had long been a common method for holding logs in a fireplace and were an essential part of the design. But as the use of coal increased, the fire grate, or iron basket, would become a more useful and effective method for holding fuel. They also introduced a new element to which decorative design could be added. The use of coal is additionally responsible for the widespread use of the fireplace fender, which was a safety guard preventing coal embers from spilling out onto the floor or carpets. Usually made of brass and requiring fluted air holes so as not to block needed hearth drafts, they became an added note of combined fireplace elegance and practical utility.

The 19th century was a period in which the fireplace underwent significant retooling. As the technology of mass production flourished, by mid-century fireplace mantels themselves began to be fashioned from cast iron. Foundries replicated numerous popular styles and designs with the new narrower hearths made specifically for the burning of coal. Cast iron was also employed in constructing the inside firewall of the hearth, which offered a further source of additional radiating heat. As the century progressed, fireplace surrounds became more modest and very highly influenced by the plethora of revisionist styles that were so popular throughout the era.

Another alteration, this time to traditional mantel shelves, also came to the fore in the latter half of the 19th century. The penchant for clutter among the Victorians, and their compulsion for collecting, necessitated the widening of the mantel. The popular use of mantel clocks was among the more trendy reasons for the change, but so too was the fashion for placing candles, vases, mirrors, and countless knickknacks on the mantel shelf.

The popular use of cast iron fire mantels led to new methods of ornamental application. None was more popular for the Victorians than ceramic tiling, which meant that decorative motifs and a wide array of colors could be easily set into the side panels of surrounds. It was a brilliant expression not only of popular tastes, but also of rapidly changing technologies and their application to domestic life. Once again, the fireplace remained the mirror of cultural evolution and changing lifestyles. Cast iron fire mantels were as modern as an omnibus and reflected the bold industrial spirit of the age. In many ways, they were the epitome of rising middle-class life—the great houses still burned logs and tree trunks as they had for generations, and the exuberant mantels of 18th century splendor remained emblems of an old

Left: Late 18th century hand-carved pine George III-style full fireplace mantle with historically significant provenance from the Hubbard House, Winnetka, Illinois. Paintings were traditionally hung above the mantelshelf. The hand carving makes this an extraordinary piece of woodworking, while the ornamental embellishments display the full grace of the Neo-classical. Acanthus leaves unfold down the corbels, while intricate ewers, another image from antiquity, are also carved here. The symmetry and workmanship are of the highest quality.

Center left: Late Victorian blue-gray Cararra marble Scottish mantel from Edinburgh. The simple geometric lines and circles of this piece provide it with a distinguishing modern patina. An Arts and Crafts character lingers in the rivers of color-rich veining.

Below left: This rare 19th century cast iron fireplace mantel with "Coalbrookdale" stamp, circa 1880s shows a highly refined sense of artistic embellishment that belies its industrial origins. It is the ultimate in mass production, though it can take some pride in its Coalbrookdale provenance. At Coalbrookdale, some of the highest achievements in industrial engineering and design were accomplished. It was a make of high Victorian esteem.

Right: Stone French Gothic Revival fireplace and cast iron grate and irons. The hearth is set within the limestone wall. A leaded tracery window appears on the left. Both fireplace and window were hidden for decades behind a false wall. The present homeowners had the plaster wall removed and discovered this remarkable carved stone behind it. William Morris tapestry chairs and heavy Gothic table continue the motif.

aristocratic way of life. But for city dwellers and the rising middle class, the cozy warmth emanating from their cast iron fireplace signaled the fast approach of the modern age.

The shadow and imprint of classical design is etched deeply into the character and personality of the 19th century fireplace mantel. As the century progressed in both Britain and the United States, the popularity of the classical remained, as did the taste for marble as an ostentatious material for mantel design. The Victorians, however, were big on borrowing from the past, so a wide variety of revivalist styles were also introduced through the period.

Among the more popular of these was the Gothic. It provided a rich and heavily textured application of medieval ornamentation. Stone and faux stone were used heavily in this design. The widespread interest in the artistic heritage of the Middle Ages produced an astounding array of baronial fireplace surrounds heavy with tracery vaulting and quatrefoil design, as well as an abiding reverence for all things Tudor. Hearths could resemble the portcullis of castle fortresses, or cathedral carvings and majestic royal imagery could fashion a handsome and romantic series of themes in stone. Exuberant floral motifs and emblems of chivalry also now graced the elaborate houses built at this time. Gothic design carried both a decorative

Left: An early 20th century oak fireplace mantel in the Neo-classical style, formerly used in a stately home, serves as the backdrop of an Italian bistro. Glass shelves holding liquor stock sit in what was once the hearth and wine bottles line what was once the mantelshelf. Over the years the beautiful oak was encrusted in white paint. Stripping away the many layers revealed a handsome and timeless elegance hidden beneath.

Right: A salvage tableau: Scottish elk horns, flanked by a pair of plaster medallions with relief portraits, circa 1910, loom above a late Georgian, circa 1820, hand carved English oak mantel from a Yorkshire manor house near Harrogate; on the mantel are a 1940s Art Modern mirror, a 1930s Italian table mirror, a 19th century Scottish carved red sandstone clock surround, a French Victorian gilt wood framed mirror, pair of 19th century English terra cotta crocket finials, a pair of bronze plated palm deco light scones, pair of white French wire plant holders; (foreground left) child's Edwardian chair; (center) late 19th century French electric radiator; (right) zinc Versailles box; American Eastlake chair.

importance and a deeper symbolic one as well, but it was the lasting artistic influence of the Arts and Crafts movement that was to have a far reaching and long lasting legacy in fireplace mantel design.

The Arts and Crafts movement recoiled at the widespread availability of poorly manufactured products and the loss of aesthetic nobility in the craftsmanship of the times. Its disciples urged a return to more traditional artistic values. Nowhere did they see the dwindling of quality more concretely than in the design and ornamentation of fireplace mantels and in reaction to the prominence of cast iron surrounds, the Arts and Crafts movement turned instead to rich, simple woods. It popularized exotic design themes and included a wide variety of materials in the making of fireplace surrounds. Moorish and Egyptian influences in particular spawned highly poetic designs, and floral motifs, carved by hand, were common. The use of geometric patterns in brickwork and the use of handmade tiles also brought a simple beauty to their work. In addition, the Arts and Crafts trend was responsible for the reintroduction of such warm and cozy design forms as the inglenook, which was a warm cubby hole, a revival of a Tudor era favorite. The small nook positioned the fireplace as an even more central focus of Arts and Crafts aesthetics. The inglenook fireplace could become its own small world, a place of conversation and gentility, art and companionship.

The one of a kind sensibility of Arts and Crafts manufacture created a harmony of design, ornament, and production, strengthening the internal as well as the external art in fireplace design. Its richness and warmth is highly sensual and speaks of a real appreciation of the artistry that flows from high quality, well turned elements and materials in domestic life.

Out of this tradition, a whole new modern sense of style and interior design was born—the same themes would be repeated in the dramatic, organic styling of the Art Nouveau period at the century's end. Wood had regained its modern ascendancy, and its influence was significant. At the same time in the United States, the modern designs of the Prairie School furthered the ideas of organic excellence and restraint. In the domestic interiors of Frank Lloyd Wright, the hearth enjoyed noble supremacy. It was richly expressive of a new harmony with nature, while simple designs heralded the arrival of the modern age.

As central heating became the ultimate technological expression of modernity, the fireplace should have been more and more relegated to the past, but its continued popular use demonstrates a deep relationship between family life and the fireplace. Even in a modern age of solar heating and underfloor systems, fireplaces still function as the altar of the family home and the center of domestic life.

It is fair to say that fireplaces are enjoying a tremendous renaissance. They are the most consistently popular element of architectural design purchased today for the home and the newest, most fashionable urban residence today will undoubtedly come fully equipped with at least one full fireplace. Firewood is plentiful in urban communities, where just a few years ago it might have been scarce. Homes without fireplaces, even condos and co-ops, are considered real estate economic liabilities. Fireplaces are high ticket items.

Left: A remarkable early example of salvage re-use. This early 19th century hand carved English Oak fireplace mantle was actually an 18th century door header (over door pediment). It was reborn in the early 1800s as the breastplate of this handsome mantle and stands as a refreshing and interesting proto-example of multiple design use.

Right: 19th century French blue marble fireplace mantel with marble corbels and linear carving. An elaborately designed 19th century French cast iron window guard with lily, tulip, and hyacinth motif does double time as a fire grate. It is a fine mixed use.

Any visit to a salvage center will quickly confirm the popularity of the fireplace today. As you walk around a reclamation center, you cannot miss the groups of interested fireplace mantel hunters. Some are even there with their decorators looking for the right style and the right size. It is not uncommon for homes today to have multiple fireplaces in them. They add a tremendous sense of comfort and civility and, in many ways, they are restoring what many feel is the loss of warmth and connection within the home.

Curiously, fireplaces are one of the few elements of reclaimed architectural salvage that are almost exclusively restricted to their primary function and use. They have few adaptations outside of providing a safe and convenient place in which to burn fuel for heat.

The big variety comes more in type and style of fireplace that you make use of in your home. For instance in a big, barren, brick urban loft, the very ornate, Georgian carved wood, full mantel surround would add a dramatic classical sense of beauty and elegance in what is initially a stark environment.

Or perhaps placing a fireplace in your bedroom would lend a feeling of deep comfort.

Outdoor fireplaces are becoming very popular. Install a 19th century cast iron fireplace in an area of your garden or yard. Shape it into an area in which you and your family can enjoy it, sitting out on cool fall evenings or crisp spring nights.

Gathering around the fire is a preternatural experience in humans. It must go back to the cave and the first warming moments when fire chased away the chill of evolution. Whatever the reason, we were made for sitting around a fire, for its sight, its sounds, and its pungent fragrance.

Light Fixtures and Chandeliers

When the lamp is shattered
The light in the dust lies dead
When the cloud is scattered
The rainbow's glory is shed.

P. B. Shelley

Above: Electric medical examination lamp, American, circa 1910, from a dentist's office. The four globe lamp was a tremendous advance to medical practitioners. The additional bulbs were a necessity due to the small wattage of early electrical bulbs. This is a handsome chrome and black metal trimmed piece.

Right: Two curious light fixtures. A handsome, tall Neo-classically designed candelabra with acanthus leaf motif holding six candles is juxtaposed with an industrial metal covered elbow floor lamp, circa 1950s. Both present a hearty contrast with the unframed religious painting of a Roman martyr.

Below: Regency period inspired brass three-lamp wall sconce with lyre motif, formerly used at the Theater in the Lyric Opera of Chicago, now used in a school library. The finely made library book shelving is highly complimented by the classical ornament-ation of the sconce.

Before the miracle of electricity, artificial light was a treasured resource. And like most of the resources of the world, the "haves" held light in abundance and the "have-nots" made do with meager supplies. Artificial light was a vanity for many, a display of social status and power. With disposable income, the rich could afford to have beeswax candles, the ultimate symbol of luxury, illuminating the room with soft amber light and scenting the air with honey-sweet fragrance. Among the peasantry there was just the sooty stench of burning reeds soaked in tallow, that brought a far less romantic glow to the room. For most people, a home's only light was the glow from the hearth.

The story of the development and evolution of lights and lighting is the on-going saga of finding better sources of light to brighten the night. It may be hard for us to imagine a world without uniform supplies of cheap, easily obtained light. Many people imagine the past years of history to be poetically lit by soft candles. Nothing could be further from reality. Candles were very costly before the invention of cheaper forms of candlepower than beeswax. And if you have ever attempted to do anything besides dine to the illumination of candlelight, you know the frustration and the heat involved. Basic activities are highly limited by meager lighting.

The evolutionary trail in the pursuit of better lighting travels from candles to oil lamps to gas to electricity. It is a long trail. But at every juncture, whatever form was the prevailing source of man-made light, artisans and craftsmen were able to fashion its fixtures and fittings into pleasing shapes and forms. Many of them are still popular and have never gone out of fashion

The 18th century was candle lit at best and oil lit where possible. It was the age of candle-holders, candelabras, and chandeliers. Wall sconces—fixtures that permitted candles to be hung on the wall—often mirror backed, were both fashionable and practical. Modest households used wood and iron or cheaper tin holders for their candles, while people of means employed brass and silver. Chandeliers were not very prevalent until the latter part of the century. They too evolved from brass or iron to later creations of glass and crystal. Necessity determined such and good taste embellished. Lanterns—enclosed glass containers for oil lamps and candles—were highly adaptable to exterior use. Frequently, elaborately iron-worked fencing incorporated lanterns over gates or atop fence posts, providing a place for outside lighting. Lanterns were also popular sources of light in hallways and staircases, and were frequently hung with chains to down-light areas of public use.

Cheaper forms of light burned grease and animal fats in boat-shaped containers known as Betty lamps. Fats often emitted foul odors as they burned and could easily fill a room with

Left: Cast iron chandelier from Hungary in the Arts and Crafts tradition with two black panthers as a motif, circa 1920. This fixture has strength, high craftsmanship, and remarkable artistic design.

Right: Imaginative front counter sculptures at Chicago's Salvage One designed by artist Daivide Nanni. Ceiling chandeliers, right, and hanging lamp, left, are extraordinary examples of salvage creativity. The round drums used as the base for the counters and the center drum used in a fountain were once used in a Wales textile mill in the late 19th century. The countertops are joined to the drums by used conduit and brass chains.

unpleasant smoke. The great watershed in the development of world lighting came at the end of the 18th century with the creation of the Argand lamp, named for the Swiss inventor Aime Argand. His work revolutionized interior lighting. The lamp, also known as the colza lamp, utilized the burning of a hollow wick that gave more direct oxygen to the flame, hence its brighter light. The lamp was lit and fueled by rapeseed oil. Nothing had ever burned as bright as Argand's lamp. One lamp was said to have the power of ten candles. The rapeseed oil was efficient and clean, and best of all lacked an offensive odor, so it was not long before this was a preferred lamp of choice. In the better households, the lamps began to exhibit a high artistic quality in their design, often employing the classical shape and character of ancient Greece or Rome like so many other fittings of the day. The bright light made indoor nighttime activities far easier and more enjoyable and lamps were hung in lanterns, set into sconces and fashioned into elaborate hanging lamps. Everything and everybody was bathed in fresh light—if the household could afford it. Elaborate chandeliers also became very popular at the end of the 18th century, but they were reserved strictly for the most special of social occasions. Their shimmering blend of gilt, crystal, strings of sparkling glass beads, and beveled teardrop shards refracted the candlelight and intensified the illumination with a dancing effect. The chandelier imparted a glittering glamour to the best room in the house.

Gas was an element of far less glamour but potently more power. It became the next advance in the development of lighting, being initially used in the early decades of the 19th century. By the mid 1830s, it was available in many an advanced metropolis. Gas was the shadow maker of the Victorian age and its arrival was to the people of the day a revolutionary expression of the modernity of the times.

The use of gas altered the design of interior domestic lighting. Because it needed to be piped into each house and then into every room, gas lamps and lights were a less mobile and more fixed element. Tubes came through the wall and through the ceiling and wall bracket lamps became an ordinary fixture in the Victorian home. Tubes also brought gas into ceiling pediments that became the Victorian version of the chandelier, though far less opulent. Technology additionally altered the style of interior lamps and

Right: Scottish Art Deco ceiling fixture, circa 1920s, with leaded inlaid art glass panels in Deco design. Scottish Deco marked a high peak in the distinctive modern style. This large fixture is emblematic of the practicality and refinement of Deco design.

Far Right: This lamp has been fashioned from a sleek 1930s era sterling silver cocktail pitcher. It adds a dramatic but simple elegance and creates an easy harmony with the unframed oil portrait behind it. Silver topped bottles are a good complement to this table arrangement.

chandeliers. Brass became a very adaptable material for period lights and lamps and as chandeliers developed a new type of opulence, later in the century, it was usually brass that was the preferred material. Now, however, large balloon chimneys of opaque or colored glass surrounded the individual chandelier gas openings, giving a romantic glow to the room. Gas lighting was also highly adaptable to the creation of elegant and artistic sconces with decorative motifs and ornamental embellishment. It was clean, efficient, and effortless, bringing advancement in efforts at public lighting. Brighter lights brought brighter and safer streets and lanes.

The Arts and Crafts movement brought an enormous array of innovative and elegant lighting fixtures to the second half of the 19th century. The fashion for stained and leaded glass was very well suited for gas lamps and overhead fixtures. In America, Louis Comfort Tiffany would create the most expressive and treasured examples of leaded glass shades and lamps.

The incandescent bulb and the harnessing of electricity would prove to be the ultimate moment in the search for good lighting. By the end of the 19th century, it had revolutionized how people lived and how cities were shaped. Over the course the first decades of the 20th century, further advances in the manufacture of lighting elements perfected electric lighting and, once again, the technological advance created a whole new level of artistic opportunity that formed popular tastes.

In the 20th century, electric lighting ushered in a new utilitarian age. Artistically, electricity demanded the same generous complement of fixtures and devices and old systems of lighting were redesigned to fit the new power

source. From Art Nouveau to Art Deco, from high American Beaux Arts to sleek Modernist expression, electricity was a blank canvas encouraging artistic experimentation and design.

Today, lighting and lighting systems run the gamut of artistic design. In salvage centers they are popular and there are plentiful examples of period design. Some are among the most highly sought elements of vintage artistry and nothing is more popular than the chandelier. It is a big item and one that householders spend a lot of time searching out. Good chandeliers can be discovered, but do plan on having them totally rewired for safety. Chandeliers often come from house teardowns, but they can also be found from hotels and restaurants. It is worth being careful as there is a lot of junk out there, but also some real treasures.

With lighting you can be as creative as you like: you can do a lot with a chandelier. Not just the mega money ones, but the less expensive, glitzy, over-the-top glass bead rococo style. Try using one as it is. Don't have it rewired, use candles. Or don't hang it in your house, put it out in the garden, or on your porch. Hang it from a tree limb, or over a table outside. Small chandeliers can easily be hung on big birdcage holders. Another suggestion is to hang a really good chandelier very low over your dining room table, at eye level. If the craftsmanship is really worthy, put it where it can be seen. You will be able to talk around it, especially at a round table.

Another wonderful, and currently very popular, source of lighting is commercial fixtures. Of course they work well in large open loft areas, but you can also use them in your kitchen or your bathroom. If you have a very

ornate room—lots of gilt, eclectic period furniture and that "Oxford Don's room look"—use a high tech fixture from a factory or a bakery. Commercial makes a great adaptation to domestic.

Another very edgy way to utilize light fixtures is to affix several long neck lighting pieces to a piece of piping, the rustier the better. Then place large pieces of mirror in strategic spots on the ceiling. Turn the necks of the light fixtures up to direct the light to the mirrors. It creates a great bounced light. Use a wide variety of long neck styles.

In contemporary designs mixed use is best. Blend lamps and lighting styles. Find contrasting fixtures and boldly use them. For example, lamps from the 1950s are always great to blend in. Their clunky modernist look is a sturdy ally in shaping a great interior. Lighting is important and a most valuable tool in design. "Light is art."

Above: Crystal quartz and brass English wall sconce, circa 1820s, re-wired for electrical use. The use of the crystal teardrops is more than purely decorative. The glass served as a refracting device to intensify the power of the light in an age when every little bit helped. Sconces were an imaginative way in which to introduce light within a room. They spread light around a large room in which a central chandelier often could not sufficiently extend light.

Left: Six French Empire sconces, early 19th century, with bronze lion head brackets and frosted "flambeau" lights. These lamps have been wired for electricity and contemporary use. Their neo-classical form is influenced by the linear design common in Greek antiquity that was so appealing to the French in the elegant Age of Napoleon.

Left: French Second Empire brass floor lamp with cherubic motif, electrified for contemporary use. This stately lamp was expressive of the exuberance of French style following the re-establishment of Bonaparte's Imperial throne in the mid 1850s. Second Empire values relished in the return of glory to the nation's life. The style made grandeur popular again.

Urns

Can storied urn or animated bust
Back to its mansion call the fleeting breath?

Thomas Gray

Above: This late-19th century French cast iron urn demonstrates the craftsmanship and popularity of iron garden material. None was more popular than the robust styles and designs executed by the French.

Right: Oversized 19th century French garden urn used in domestic American interior. Whimsically this urn is filled not with greenery but with French silk pillows instead. It sits atop a contemporary enamel and burnished nickel stand in the Art Nouveau style that complements the contemporary stairway.

Below: Early 1900s American cast iron urn in a simple cup shape. American foundries produced these urns in large numbers as the passion for gardening reflected a growing popular taste.

No object of classical antiquity has so held the popular favor and is so practical as the urn. Its use goes back to the world of the Caesars, and urns have framed the landscapes and gardens of history with exquisite ornament since. Essentially vessels to contain important materials, urns were very much a part of the restrained decoration of the ancient world, where their design projected a sense of form and refinement. These delightful objects graced the Roman villa of Hadrian and the courtyards of Athens. Urns adorned buildings in the Forum of Trajan and ornamented the roofline of the Coliseum. Their silhouette was a mark of beauty in countless niches and on endless pedestals. Their curvaceous shape was held to replicate the female torso among the ancients. Throughout the ancient world they displayed a symmetry and proportion that reflected a larger grandeur—nature's own.

Italians have two words to describe the urn—urne and vasi. Urns basically come in two classical shapes and sizes. The first is said to resemble an ancient low Greek cup, tezza in Italian. The second is said to resemble a tall Greek vase, much the shape of a large rounded bell, campana in Italian, bell-shape or cup-shape. Campana or tezza, all urn shapes have their origins in these two basic classical forms.

Even at the farthest reaches of the Roman Empire, the national character could be seen in the abiding pleasure Roman people took in the aesthetic beauty of the urn. It was a symbol of sophisticated bearing, a vestige of the larger prestige of Roman influence and good taste. A fundamentally functional object, it was the subject of great embellishment. Urns could be inscribed with tableaus of heroic exploits or scenes to pay homage to the gods. They might display emblems of the State or show the important characters of history. Urns grew to be an all-inclusive art form.

Urns were so much part of the spirit of the ancient world that they have had a powerful influence upon many subsequent centuries. It is why they continue to have use even in later times. During the Renaissance, for instance, they were rediscovered in the ruins of antiquity and became a staple of Italian gardens. Their prominent use in ancient times, and reuse in the present, was seen to be a connection to the flavor and ideals of a bygone age. No one used urns with more dramatic style than Louis XIV in the building of Versailles. The great bronze urns he commissioned for his gardens were testament to the grandeur of his country palace, which rivaled even that of Rome.

When further discoveries of antiquity began to be unearthed in abundance during the 18th century, the artistic excellence of Rome and Greece delighted the sensibilities of Europe, particularly in England. And nothing unearthed in the archeological digs of the times, in such wondrous places as Pompeii and Herculaneum, brought more joy than the discovery of the prominent use of urns in the aesthetic lives of the past. In the world of the 18th century, urns appeared tailor made

for the many refined gardens that were so much a part of the expanding array of great country houses.

Urns, once again, became the bearers of precious materials—the lush exotic greenery of classically designed gardens. Urns afforded not only a richly ornamental display of cascading flowers and vines, they also vividly mirrored the sculptured beauty that was so much a part of the period's new harmony with nature. Urns framed walks and paths. They sat atop garden walls and balustrades lifting nature high. Urns sat imperiously at entrance gates and the porticoed entries of majestic homes. Fitted into the boxwood niches of hedges, they gilded the excess of nature with extra abundance.

Generally made of stone or marble, urns were heavy and very costly. But with the coming of the technology of mass production in the mid 19th century, the Victorian age's use of the urn multiplied quickly. Cast iron became an element that enhanced the durability and affordability of urns. The various shapes and sizes and their heavily layered ornamental decoration made cast iron urns a decidedly elegant addition to Victorian garden fashion. Urns complemented the Victorians' love for gardening, and the spirit of garden embellishment and the trade catalogues of iron manufacturers and foundries were full of different designs to satisfy the public demand. In America, manufacturers also introduced a wide variety of styles, many of

which did not come from the authentic classical forms of the ancient world. Invention and popular tastes redefined both the character and the fashion of urns. In addition, American botanicals provided an exuberant selection of plants with which to fill them.

By the turn of the century, terra cotta (Italian for baked earth) became a very popular material in the production of urns as it could be glazed and fashioned with remarkable detail. This was a shift that carried well into the 20th century and accounts for the current popularity of terra cotta elements in garden design.

Urns enjoy wide movement and a primacy of place in salvage centers today. Cast iron urns are, by their nature, durable and, therefore, both available and highly prized. They add an immediate grace to any area in which they are placed. In any style of home, urns reshape the environment. Filled with a variety of lush foliage, they transform their surroundings. Urns reinvigorate entryways and stairways. They frame the symmetry of steps in any garden or walkway and bring unity and connection between a house and its surroundings—so use them with abandon. Best of all, urns help to rearrange the shape of things around you, especially the outside. The ancient Romans, after all, used them to control nature, making them spaces for small but beautiful gardens that could be placed anywhere and carefully cultivated.

Right: This enormous, oversized, 19th century French cast iron urn contains its own elaborate variety of garden, thick with brilliant early growth. The distressed finish adds to the romance and the drama of this piece set against a wall of hedge adding explosive color and pulling the eye to its spectacular placement.

Left: Garden panorama. This extraordinary modern American garden reflects the aesthetics and grandeur of English refinements. Large cast iron urns are brimming with French sage and frame a view beyond the red brick walls replete with finials fashioned of delicate brick pieces. A wheelbarrow and garden tools attest to the activity of gardening underway. A forest of handsome trees shape the contours of this lush perspective.

If you have a wide-open space, consider using urns in pairs, really big campana urns, to frame a view. Step back from your house. Get its perspective. Then let the urns become a border for the view.

If you have several tezza urns, the cup-shaped smaller ones, use them on your dining table. Run them down the middle. The more lush, the better. Bring them in from the garden and plop them down.

Use urns in different rooms. If you find a tall cast iron urn and pedestal, you can have it made into a bathroom sink quite easily. The plumbing pipes and the drain will fit through the base and the faucets can be wall mounted. You can have a copper liner made for the sink or use very trendy glass.

Urns translate into fountains with great adaptability. Have the water mechanism installed, and you are in business.

Urns can be filled with collectables. Large colored ornaments are good. So are tennis balls or a thirty-pound sack of candy corn. Try shoes, balls of yarn, or rolled up towels. It is a look.

Large urns can be used in your living room. Fill them with large, exotic French silk pillows instead of plants.

Keep a large urn on hand to be filled with large foliage like tree branches, tall flowers, and the branches of blooming fruit trees. The Carlisle Hotel in New York has an extraordinary dining room design by the late Mark Hampton. At the center of the room stands a 360-degree tapestry banquette and six tables. Above the diners, atop the banquette center, is a huge urn always filled with lush lilies and tree branches or other majestic floral extravagancies. You can do this at home. Anywhere.

Right: An Asian terra cotta urn complements the lines and textures in this grand Japanese domestic residence. Terra cotta roof tiles expand the theme of handsome baked earth simplicity.

Left: This glazed Asian terra cotta urn holds an array of remarkable walking sticks and is well matched with not only the exotic furniture but the lines and fashion of the room.

Right: This urban garden sits in the midst of a highly classical court, echoing high Neo-classical touches of design and form. This Chicago pied-a-terre is a blend of styles. The mid-19th century cast iron, highly detailed English urns spill over with color and fragrance set around the ground cover and cobbles.

Left: This large terra cotta Mediterranean olive jar stands on the rolling lawn of an American garden, adding a distinctive touch of resourceful antiquity.

Below: Early 20th century tazza-form cast iron urn (Greek Kylix style) and pedestal. Its refined design was very popular and iron construction made its mass production and availability an easy reality, contrasting with the more expensive and harder to obtain marble versions of the original.

Kitchen Items, Stoves, and Sculleries

Kissing don't last: cookery do!

George Meredith

Above: Four-legged, 19th century Northern French, cast iron wood burning stove and oven with ceramic tile front. The highly decorative finish expresses a remarkable elegance of early Arts and Crafts. The stove also demonstrates the ongoing technological advancement in household appliances.

Right: A classic 1950s American double oven gas range has its own special timeless beauty and utility. It is the Cadillac of kitchen appliances. This big four-burner, replete with center griddle and double broilers was once the top-of-the-line. Today, its design retains its bold and attractive innovative utility in a kitchen that is both highly functional and cozy.

Below: French Art Deco butcher's block, circa 1920s. The elaborate yet refined motif of carvings are hallmarks of Art Deco rounded linearism. This is an example of an age-old implement reflecting a highly styled and popular avant-garde fashion. This is not merely a decorative piece. It is heavy duty and professional.

Kitchens have always had a unique influence on domestic living. Their connection to the everyday lives of real people is without rival. Historically, however, kitchens have not always been the cozy focal point of family life so familiar to most people today. In earlier centuries, among the affluent, kitchens were more the domains of household staff, whose responsibility it was to prepare the family meal. Far more primitive and cumbersome than we are used to today, kitchens then were disconnected from the householder's family. Meals were never served in the room in which they were prepared and little separated the technology available to noble or peasant. Kitchens among the well-to-do were usually larger to accommodate the number of workers needed for the tasks involved. Food was cooked in great hearths. In them, large joints of meat or fowl were usually spit roasted over wood fires. Cooking pots hung over open flames or embers from iron hooks. More ordinary families, which usually meant poor, endured a much more simple place for culinary preparations. Food was usually cooked in one pot over an open hearth that doubled as the family heating system. Often the kitchen was part of one large room that served a multiplicity of family needs. Ovens, principally the domain of bakers, eventually offered opportunity for cooking beyond the usual loaves. But ovens were costly and available only to the very rich. Cooking was labor intensive, heavy work—the storage, preparation, and many tasks involved made it an all day job.

Despite the long history of primitive kitchen technology and design, evolution did eventually arrive. With the coming of the industrial age in the late 18th century and the advances made in developing new uses for iron, the open hearth gave way to more convenient methods of cooking like the cast iron stove. Iron was capable of containing heat sources and channeling heat in ways that until then had been impossible. Though early iron stoves and cookers had little temperature control, constant attention made it possible to cook in an entirely new fashion. Iron plates located on the flat surface of the stove allowed cooking with pots on the top of a stove, advancing their utility even further. While primitive to our modern standards, this was a big improvement.

It was the Victorians who really advanced the technology of the kitchen. The unprecedented inventiveness of the second half of the 19th century brought about huge leaps in refinements in gadgetry and engineering. The availability of coal introduced a new and more dependable fuel source, while emerging scientific influences began to calibrate cooking appliances and introduce reliable systems of temperature control and measurement, aiding cooks everywhere. With the gradual rise of the middle class, due also to the influence of industrialization, the kitchen began to evolve into the heart of the home, into the family center that we know it as in our own time. Family meals, by many, were now eaten in the family kitchen. This was especially true in households without kitchen staff. By the end of World War I, the availability of inexpensive household employees was coming to an end and would further the custom for many of kitchen eating.

Left: This vintage 1890s American four-burner cast iron "Jewel" brand gas stove, presently doubling as a library table, actually still functions. In this eclectic Chicago Gold Coast pied-a-terre it holds a 19th century Italian book press, an 18th century cathedral pediment, assorted art books, and copy of a David's head. Though the warming oven holds storage, it still can cook an omelet.

Right: A trio of hand-hammered copper, double-handled chocolate melting vats, from a commercial candy company. Each sits atop a three-legged industrial stand from another commercial enterprise. They do, however, appear to be a perfect match and offer an opportunity for inventiveness beyond their previous confection cooking.

in architecture and furniture reflected the popular tastes and fashions of the day, so too did the elements used in the kitchen life and design. For instance, in France by the late 19th century, cast iron kitchen stoves began to accrue the addition of fancy decoration such as tiles and stylish design motifs. Utility began to be complemented by the introduction of well-crafted artistry. The application of aesthetic principles, that is the attempt to bring beauty as well as function to the design of kitchen apparatus, found keen interest among the public. Affluence and the opportunities brought by the transitions initiated during the industrial age changed many areas of ordinary life. Cities underwent enormous growth in America during the late 19th century. Large numbers of immigrants came from Europe expanding the urban populations of the nation. This growth, especially among the middle class, brought a development in how people lived. City people had different needs from country folk. Urban living was reshaping the necessities of life. Eating styles changed as well. The manner in which people prepared their food underwent massive changes also.

Cities became centers of the move to modernity. Though many were filled with large numbers of urban poor, cities also began to shape the lifestyles of its more prosperous residents. Efficient homes were begetting more efficient modes of living. Before the end of the century, electricity galvanized America, and the stunning inventions of men like Thomas Edison were reconfiguring domestic tastes. The icebox evolved into the refrigerator through such inventiveness, and the stove transformed into the electric range.

Nowhere was the spirit of American inventiveness more apparent than in the kitchens of the nation's households. Perhaps no other room in the home underwent such amazing and rapid change as the kitchen. The 20th century introduced not only new gadgets, but also a new sense of practicality in the kitchen. From toasters to juicers and from coffeepots to griddles, electricity and the cleverness of exuberant American inventors found exciting applications for science in everyday life. The kitchen underwent remarkable development in the process. It was a new age of kitchen productivity.

Further advances in plumbing and public sanitation altered the scope of what it was possible for the kitchen to become. When water no longer had to be physically carried from an outside water source, but rather could be pumped inside a home's kitchen, it signaled a major breakthrough. In the 20th century with the development of the tap bringing water through underground pipes at the turn of a knob, arm-wearied cooks were provided with an indispensable element of kitchen modernity. Kitchens grew to become less and less the messy scullery of intensive preparation that they once were. The coming of the refrigerator railroad car in America, meant that meat and other foodstuffs became more uniform and family meals became more practical. Cooking was decidedly not the grueling task it once was. The transition of the domestic kitchen and the evolution of kitchen technology altered the lifestyle of the world. Everything from rolling pins and spatulas to cooking stoves and tin sinks found fresh attention in the growing modernity of kitchen life.

There is an old story that claims that traditional English plum pudding became a popular holiday dessert in the mid 19th century because it could easily be cooked by steaming it on the top of the family stove. Ovens in domestic stoves, at the time, were still too unpredictable. Cakes were strictly the province of the local baker. Ovens lacked sufficient dependability until further refinements made them more exacting.

But once kitchens began to make serious technological and scientific advances, they underwent a secondary, but no less important, transition in their external design. In the same way that ornamentation and stylistic detail

Kitchens, over the past 150 years, have evolved into warm centers of family living in most ordinary households. They mirror a family centered ethos that developed in the expanding, middle class, Victorian-era households. In the kitchen, families gathered for their daily meals. They sat around the table together sharing their food and their common bond. Kitchen furniture soon began to reflect the changing nature of kitchen purpose and necessity. Table designs and shapes expressed a universal reality that strengthened the practical ability of the family to come together as one. Large sturdy tables allowed whole households to gather. In addition, they often doubled as a work area for baking, food

Below left: This kitchen work area is enhanced by the addition of a dramatic metal horse's head complete with leather blinders. This well placed decorative piece adds a clever touch of the country.

Below: This German cast iron stove, circa 1788, is a fine example of the technological advances of the 18th century and the popular taste for Neo-classical decorative design. The double handled urn pediment on the top is representative of the popular style of embellishment. So too are the classical swag motifs that are repeated on the front panels. Familiar Greek key design enhances the entire stove. The center oval was utilitarian as well as decorative. It permitted heat to radiate more evenly.

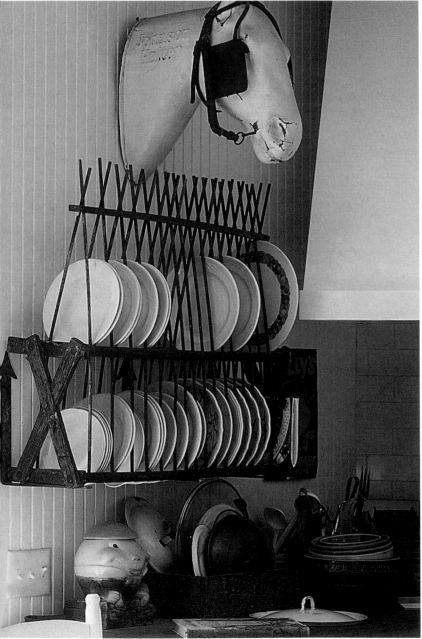

preparation, or more elaborate cooking projects that were essential to on-going family life and routine. As styles of cooking became more varied and elaborate, the elements of kitchen life began to expand. The kitchen moved into an age of accessorizing.

As kitchens became a more functioning part of family life, their embellishment and ornamentation also became more decorative and reflective of domestic living. The storage of foodstuffs and perishables introduced new devices for protection of things like sugar, flour, and salt. The use of more elaborate condiments in cooking brought the use of spice racks and cabinetry to house their containers, while also doubling in some instances for the storage of dishware and pots and pans. Inventive crock ware and glazed pottery gave further design elements to kitchens and they remain valuable items of utility and beauty. Pie safes and cheese cabinets joined a growing array of cast iron skillets and copper stockpots that were essential equipment in the well-stocked kitchen.

Today, some of the equipment from long ago kitchens might appear a step back, technologically, in modern utility and practical necessity. But the singular styles and designs in craftsmanship and inventiveness still hold much beauty and charm. While not many can afford the commitment of time and energy that a wood burning cast iron stove might necessitate, stone or hammered tin sinks remain as functional as they are elegant. The wide variety in fine English and American wooden farmhouse or factory tables bring a piece of the past into the present. Butcher block and marble top surfaces bear the strains of time with unusual success and are readily available. Large copper kettles and soup pots remain as functional as they are chic, and good cooks know their value. The utility of brass and copper kitchen equipment never loses its edge even after a century of use. Contemporary kitchens have never been more modern, with convection ovens, microwaves, and eight burner professional stoves on the top of most decorators' lists of trendy equipment. But cooking is essentially chemistry, the application of heat at measured intervals that transforms raw foodstuffs into remarkably savory meals. For cooks with talent and invention, the excitement of fine cuisine is enhanced by equipment of aesthetic sensibilities and the allure of historical design. There is no grander magic than making an omelet on a 100-year-old gas burning stove.

Kitchens, for many individuals, mean uniformity of design and a maximum of utility and ease. But for others, kitchens are about romance and creativity. They are about wire whisks and French copper bowls, domed Amish pie screens, and salads made in eighty-year-old Chinese rice baskets and served on a 200-year-old Irish monastery table while sitting on unmatched chairs from a 1940s Parisian café. In relishing the grandeur of the past, we have treasure and beauty in the present.

Left: Modern high tech American renovated domestic kitchen with white enamel tile walls and classic red metal Coca-Cola machine, circa 1947. Above is the familiar Coca-Cola neon sign from the 1940s. Both items add an important touch of the past to this restaurant style, nickel plate detailed room.

Baths and Bathroom Furniture

Moab is my wash-pot; over Edom I will cast out my shoe.

Psalm 60:8

Above: The dramatic age of Art Nouveau meets Art Deco and inspires this tulip-shaped white porcelain bathroom sink, circa 1910. The curving sculptured form of this elegant piece is timeless.

Right: A pair of burnished steel French dentist's office swivel chairs with tripod bases, circa 1940, representing the ultimate in cool, sophisticated utilitarian techno-modernity. They complement the mosaic interior of this modern Roman-style domestic bath.

Below: French claw-footed free standing four-sided metal bath, circa 1890s. This tub incorporates the French popular taste for bathtubs in the center of the room. Plumbing was not directly attached to the bathtub; instead water was run through pipes that attached away from the walls.

By the second half of the 19th century, the inventiveness of the industrial age had unleashed countless wonders and gadgets that reflected the cleverness of the times and brought new conveniences to the home. Science and engineering were truly creating a fresh modern age. And while many devices relieved the burden of excess labor for many, nowhere was this advance in technology more of a welcome reality than in the bathrooms of domestic life. Sanitation and hygiene were growing components of this modern passage. Cities exploded, developing large new populations. But a sad fact of their rapid expansion was the heightened incidence of disease and death provoked by poor sanitation. The seriousness with which the Victorians engaged this issue was born out by the development, on a massive scale, of water and sanitation facilities to protect populations and provide a healthier environment.

Perhaps the most wondrous advancement of the Victorian era was the development of the "water closet." The water flushed toilet seemed to catapult society into new age of civility. Ironically, it was actually more of a rediscovery of the technology, since it is recorded that the ancient Minoans had a device similar to the water-flushing toilet as far back as 1700 B.C. How this piece of ancient technology could have been lost for more than 3,000 years is among one of the great mysteries of life. Though the engineering of the toilet was in use on a limited scale through the 18th century, it was the Victorians who made it a necessity for everyone. With the coming of the water closet to the ordinary lives of everyday people, in the second half of the 19th century, the world became a different place. Gradually, people began to abandon the privies and earth closets of the backyard for the comfort, convenience, and sanitary health of the inside toilet. This addition to the family home challenged the architectural and stylistic inventiveness of the times as well.

At the same time as toilets grew into a more common usage, technology also brought about a significant change in other areas of personal hygiene with the development of convenient bathing facilities within the home. With the introduction of piped or "plumbed" water into people's homes, bathing grew to be far removed from the laborious effort that it once was. Even in the finest houses, before the development of the basic features of plumbing, each bath would have to be filled by hand, bucket by bucket. In the 18th century, bathing was still a rare indulgence, thought by many to be unhealthy at best. But as common sense prevailed, elaborate copper and zinc baths came to stand in elegant and fashionable salons. It was a luxury, however, that required the efforts of servants to prepare, assist, and then remove. Among the poor, bathing was seldom an option, except on only the most necessary of occasions. It would take the Victorians to fabricate the intricate systems of pressurized pipes necessary to carry water from central water mains into ordinary homes. The ability to control running water changed the way people lived. Bathtubs could be filled from taps. Toilets could be flushed. Sewage could be channeled away from critical sources of drinking water preventing contamination. Such innovative feats of engineering stopped the

Left: This grand Edwardian porcelain bath tub is eminently simple in its design, but both practical and efficient in its luxurious form. Deep and well fashioned, it is the perfect complement to gilded swan faucets and Gothic Revival appointments of mirrors and a niche of shelves holding bath products. The sconces and side pediments add to the castle-like feel of this splendid room.

Right: This simple rectangular bath is enhanced by the addition of this fine marble encasement that provides architectural style and efficiency. The rich motif from the side panel is repeated in the triangular framed architectural artifact hung above the tub.

At Luttrellstown Castle in County Dublin, a castellated monster of a house, once home to a branch of the famous Irish brewers the Guinness family, a mark of their past refinements and civility can be seen in the grand hand-hammered copper bathtub that connects to a prototype copper and brass water heater that looks very much like a still. Its dramatic early Regency elegance and aristocratic inventiveness remain an icon of the age of discovery when intelligence and wealth sought to tame the environment of everyday life by the application of creative science. Though the technology is complicated and even dangerous, and the steps to draw a hot bath egregiously complicated, the apparatus still works today. If elegance were the only principle of modern bathroom design, Luttrellstown Castle would have no rival. But its eccentric beauty is no match for the simple turn of the tap marked hot.

The modern bathroom as Victorians knew it is much the same as we know today. Victorians rid themselves of the old tin baths of the generation preceding them, pre-

downward spiral of urban health and sanitation, and set human beings on the road to "that fresh scrubbed feeling" of modernity. With further refinements in the methods for the heating of water, technology was altering the frequency and ease with which the family bathed.

Gradually the home was being rethought to accommodate the most important addition to its design since the development of glass windows. The bathroom became a reality of modern 19th century living. And, like all other aspects of domestic necessity, it was not long before the pragmatic and the mundane began to reflect the aesthetics of the times. There was no reason that this new room could not reflect the tastes and styles of times. So with their familiar passion for elegant excess, Victorians took the bathroom to themselves and embellished its functionality with elegance, luxurious fashion, and continued refinements of taste.

ferring copper or zinc for their fashionable rolled top designs. They were attracted to the elegance and convenience of footed baths often bearing styles featuring the feet of beasts and mythic creatures that were lasting elements of the Gothic Revival style. Baths were made from easily obtainable cast iron and lined with creamy white porcelain or luxurious enamels. Cast iron exteriors were always painted and offered a variety of options that easily produced fashionably contrasting bath decors. The Victorians' heightened sensitivity to sanitation and good order also made wood cabinetry popular. The encasing of the bath, the toilet, and the washbasin in attractive woods was primarily a health concern but soon became a popular decorating feature.

The washbasin had a long and fashionable evolution in domestic use. It was among the last pieces of modern bathroom furniture to reach its final

Left: A remarkable Art Deco white marble bathroom sink with dramatic acrylic legs by designer Sam Marx. It came from one of Chicago's most well known vintage Art Deco residential buildings and could easily become the anchor of a new and more eclectic bath.

Right: This late-19th century footed cast iron English bathtub is the centerpiece of a fresh bathscape and is complemented by the deco vanity cabinet, wicker chair, and glazed terra cotta decorative fish

form. Long before the first pipes broke through a bathroom wall to connect the taps for modern washbasins, the large familiar jug and bowl sitting on the washstand of many bedrooms served as the prototype of the bathroom sink. Before washing with soap and hot water on a daily basis became a regular feature of everyday life, a few splashes from the standing water of the bedroom pitcher was all the hygiene most people desired. Water jugs enjoyed a long history of use and were highly decorative by the time that plumbed pipes first brought running water into the family bathroom. With the added luxury of abundant hot water ready at the turn of the tap, the ever-vigilant advocates of home hygiene had an important ally in the advent of the bathroom sink.

Washbasins were an easy complement for the other features of bathroom design. Whether they were cast iron molded basins, wall-mounted in the vogue of the late 19th century, elaborate free standing porcelain sinks mounted upon classical columns, or elegant painted bowls encased in heavy tooled mahogany cabinetry, the convenience and functional utility of the washbasin were valuable additions to domestic life.

The interior space of bathroom walls and flooring began to reflect the utility of their everyday purpose. The introduction of ceramic tiles in particular proved to be most efficient. Easily cleaned and maintained with a maximum of attention to sanitary details, tiles became an elegant fashion enhancing the new aesthetics of bathroom design. In popular Victorian and

Edwardian vogue, tiles could be used in practical application with wallpapers, being often used around the lower, more moist-prone portions of bathroom walls, while patterned paper covered the upper portions. An adapting public was quickly learning to use the best methods of design for the newest and now most indispensable room in the house.

As domestic bathrooms grew in popularity during the late 19th century, it was only to be expected that they would reflect the substantial influences of the period's architectural and artistic styles. The grandeur of Art Nouveau appeared tailor made for the blending of art and technology. At the same time, the simplicity and utility of the Arts and Crafts movement lent itself well to the sanitary utilitarianism of developing modern bathrooms.

The last word in modern bathroom fashion has been luxury and comfort for quite some time. Since the beginning of the 1930s, America's high emphasis on health and hygiene has had an over-riding influence on the styles and fashions in bathroom design. Even with the strong popular attraction that reclaimed architectural salvage holds for many in the design and reconstruction of old homes little interest can be found for the recycling and reuse of vintage toilets. Environmentally, they use far too much water in their everyday function. In many areas of the country modern "low-flo" toilets stressing the economical use of water are a must. There appears to be little large-scale interest in used toilets. However, with only this exception, bathroom furniture from the past is enjoying a tremendous resurgence.

During the 1920s and 1930s, there was a strong influence of industrial aesthetics in domestic bathrooms. Bathrooms were undergoing a concerted effort to shed the more elaborate embellishments of the Victorian and Edwardian periods. The emphasis was on technology, design, and materials. Bathrooms were becoming more compact by the 1930s, and crisp modern utility was an important design device. During this era in the United States, toilet water tanks began to disappear from their prominent

place high above the toilet and were more popularly attached to the back of the toilet itself. Such streamlining also was responsible for the popularity of non-footed, boxed-in style bathtubs. Showers had enjoyed wide popularity since the beginning of the century, and by the 1930s, they were eclipsing the more traditional tubs, appearing more and more in domestic use. Many believe they reached their ultimate in luxury and design in the enormous "hub-cap" style English showerheads, made famous in five star hotels, and encasing the user in extravagant cascades of water. Mirrored medicine cabinets also evolved to become an indispensable component of bathroom life. In addition to ordering and organizing countless bathroom necessities, mirrors themselves were utilized with more ingenuity in modern bathroom design. The remarkable streamlined modernity of the Art Deco style lent itself naturally to bathroom mirror fashions. The timelessness and high functionality of such fancy glass cabinetry makes it a style that never fades.

The introduction of nickel, brass, and chrome for ordinary use in domestic bathroom faucets, nozzles, knobs, and showerheads over the decades built upon the technological notions of Victorian designers. Little improvement has been necessary beyond minor changes in fashion or style. Even today, the basic utility of such designs is in continuous use. While reproduction of such styles is very popular today, hardware from the past is readily available and holds up to reuse in contemporary homes.

Today, practicality remains an important feature of modern bathroom use. Many homes have multiple bathrooms to the extent that would have surprised thrifty Victorians. But function and utility do not eclipse the aesthetic in modern bathrooms. The allure of styles from textured exuberance of revival styles to the minimalist simplicity of the modern continues to enhance and ornament a very basic necessity of life.

Left: This highly imaginative bath setting has a vintage late-Victorian style in the large pub mirror that rises over the modern enameled tub encased in rich cherry wood that complements the mirror frame. The dark wall treatment and the carpets, together with the two porcelain lamps with shades, create a bath space that is comfortable and clubby.

Right: A vintage porcelain pedestal bathroom sink, circa 1910. The classical inspired pedestal column has a touch of the revivalist spirit that was still a prevalent artistic style in America before World War I. In this modern mosaic powder room, this touch of antiquity is complementary.

Iron Gates and Ornamental Metalwork

Right against the eastern gate,
Where the great sun begins his state.

John Milton

Iron is a unique metal and has been a valued staple of civilized cultures since ancient times. The process of its extraction from mineral ore and the arduous labor leading to its eventual production often changed the balance of power in the world. Armies rode to victory on the military application of its uses. Iron was the nuclear energy of antiquity. Its strength and utility were without equal. Wrought iron was iron manufactured in the forge by the brute strength of the smith with a hammer and an anvil. His place in the life of a town or village was central in the age preceding industrialization. His work fashioned specialized pieces with strict utilitarian purpose, each item hand made, unique, the craft of his artistry. From horseshoes to nails, from weathervanes and belt buckles to iron railings, the work of the smith was slow-paced and intense. Iron mongering was a noble profession, more necessary for many than the services of a primitive physician.

In the Georgian era, the working of iron for the elaborate entrance gates and property barriers in the many great country houses that were constructed during the period became an important part of the livelihood of the smith. Indeed, many larger estates employed their own smiths to make the necessary iron products for the house. With iron, architects could design decorative gates of scale and proportion to complement the magnificence of a country residence. Gates were the first extension of the house to greet the visitor. Their imposing grandeur gave a foretaste of the character and prestige of the house that lay within. In domestic interiors, wrought iron work became a popular and highly decorative medium for stairway balustrades. Iron could bend and curl and bow in a highly stylized fashion, yet with delicate looking classical motifs. The fashionable 18th century architectural designer, Robert Adams, framed his elegant urban doorways in smart London houses with ironwork railings and created a new taste for the graceful application of the metal. During this same period, the very first iron bridge in England was built across the Severn River in Shropshire, demonstrating a further use for this malleable metal. Further uses for ironwork multiplied during the Regency period with the introduction of hooded iron balconies and decorative window hooding that added extensive ornamentation to city homes. The introduction of terraced housing multiplied the opportunity for the use of iron decorative design and soon became all the rage. Railings and gates were becoming commonplace, providing a certain urban safety as well as beauty in their use.

While the artistry of the Georgian era created iron ornamentation of exquisite symmetry and hand wrought quality, it is really the Victorians who make their era another age of iron. Cast Iron. Industrialization expanded the processing methods and use of iron, manufacturing it cheaply and in abundance. The introduction of cast iron, made by pouring molten metal into premade forms changed the face of Victorian life. And with the further development of industrial iron works,

Left: Two pairs of early-20th century cast iron columns without embellished capitals have an Art Deco symmetry about them, flanking a pair of 20th century American iron driveway gates. In the foreground rests an Art Deco limestone bovine carving once used at the Bowman Dairy. Matching cast stone urns sit on either side.

Right: A tableau of industrial age ironwork in the salvage yard: (lower center) English Arts and Crafts wrought iron gate; (lower left) English Victorian iron newel post; (right) fragment of 19th century Scottish cast iron widow's walk from the Glasgow foundry of Walter McFarland; (center) curved decorative piece of red wrought iron; (left) English Victorian cast iron roof cresting; (right) 19th century American cast iron roof cresting with corn motif; (top) 19th century Arts and Crafts inspired cast iron fence from Oxford.

"Coalbrookedale" is a name that still rings with history and invention. To many, this once small town in England is the birthplace of the Industrial Revolution. There, iron was first forged in a furnace during the early years of the 18th century. The proximity of a good supply of coal and water made it an ideal site for what was the world's first modern iron works. Coalbrookedale manufactured many remarkable items for domestic use. (Their signature stoves are still made.) During the Great Exhibition of 1851, when the inventiveness of the Victorian age was on view for visitors from all over the world, Coalbrookedale managed to capture the attention of all with an extraordinary set of cast iron gates that dazzled the crowds. Today those remarkable gates can still be seen in London's Hyde Park. The

factories created for the large-scale fabrication of iron and iron products, the small-scale operation of the village smith became restricted to the repair of iron elements, horseshoes, and carriage wheels. Iron would define the character and versatility of the Victorian age and signaled its passage to a new modernity.

With iron readily available, it was soon a creative and integral part of the redevelopment of many large urban centers such as London, Paris, and New York. The famous architectural engineering firm of Brunnel and Wyatt changed the face of London with iron. Their extraordinary cast iron construction of Paddington Railway Station, in the 1850s, demonstrated not only the brawn of iron but also its ability to permit highly decorative and delicate ornamentation. Cast iron lamp posts soon became a part of the urban landscape. With high imagination and a great sense of whimsy, the design for the embankment along the River Thames incorporated large ornamental intertwining fish. Even the cast iron benches along the river were embellished with Victorian flair, with detailed sphinxes serving as arm rests. Cast iron was putty in the hands of architects and engineers of the day. While people were amazed at the inventions of Victorian technologies, not least of which were the railroad, the steamship, and the telephone, they also were delighted with the beauty and the elaborate ornamentation that abounded everywhere.

great contribution that cast iron has made to the architectural and artistic design has its origins in the iron works of Coalbrookedale.

With the ready availability of cast iron, the quality and ornamentation of Victorian design took off. The exteriors of domestic architecture grew in their exuberance. Roofs sported cast iron cresting with elaborate motifs. Cast iron gates could be manufactured at remarkable rates and their designs soon enhanced towns and villages across the country. Scottish iron works produced fine quality iron ornamentation that quickly restyled the exteriors of public buildings and domestic residences in Edinburgh and Glasgow, as both prospered in the wake of industrialization. Growing urban centers were enhanced by the addition of iron railings around public buildings and civic centers. Architectural pattern books made it easy for local craftsman to imitate designs that people found appealing. The architectural flow of cast iron rails and fences added a distinguished beauty to town designs. In addition they were practical and durable as well as elegant. Their framework gave definition to public thoroughfares and private lanes, giving an orderly definition to everyday life. Variety in style and design reflected the popular eclectic tastes of the day such as classical.

The growing use of ornamental ironwork created a remarkable new architectural style. Introduced by some of the finest architects of the day, such as A. W. Pugin who was responsible for so much Gothic Revival and

Left: A cast iron elevator grate from the 19th century former United States Federal Building, Chicago, designed by Henry Ives Cobb (wrecked in 1960) with eagle emblem and design motif of fleur-de-lis. Embellishment also includes the symbolic classical Roman ornamentation. A piece like this would make a striking presence on any wall, inside or out.

Right: 19th century carved American walnut Victorian Gothic Revival chair with William Morris inspired red and gold brocade upholstery. An ecclesiastical motif predominates in the three pointed pediments—bishop's miter at the top and two stylized lilies at either side. Arts and Crafts-like carvings of stylized sunflowers fill the center arch. On the wall is a wrought iron Art Nouveau panel of irises.

Left: A decidedly monastic interior is created in this open timbered great room. The wrought iron fadstool, at left, has a markedly episcopal feel and complements the tall wrought iron candelabra in the upper left. The simple carved furniture and cobbled floor have a Spanish quality. The holy icon in the above rafter and the cast iron bell complete the styling.

Below: Within this dramatically wide Chicago living room designed in the International Style, on either side of the central entrance stand Louis Sullivan's elevator grates from his Chicago Stock Exchange Building. Four examples of Mies Van der Rohe's Barcelona Chairs have their backs to the camera. To the right, a wooden chair of the Prairie School designed by Frank Lloyd Wright. Facing the camera are two black leather and chrome chairs by Le Corbusier. To the left the top portion of two leather backed dining room chairs by Wright are remnants from his Imperial Hotel in Tokyo.

ecclesiastical buildings and Sir Charles Barry, the architect of the British Houses of Parliament, the new fashion enshrined the growing use of elaborate ironwork with an enthusiasm and confidence that seemed to reflect the aggressive Victorian self-perception and sense of worth. The Arts and Crafts movement also had great interest in the decorative use of iron. While they demanded their iron to be wrought rather than cast, the fashion for metal opened an artistic outlet and they developed works of typical high quality, hand made one of a kind pieces of artistic ornament.

Because cast iron is such a durable element it stands the test of time. Many examples of High Victorian cast iron ornamentation are commonly available today. Gates made at some of Scotland's most established foundries in the late 19th century are plentiful even in American markets. They might come with rusting or distressed patinas, but to many this is an added layer of architectural character. The same is true for decorative roof cresting, finials, and newel posts that retain their period aesthetics even in our own contemporary use.

In America the use of ornamental ironwork weaved its way into the architectural ethos of the nation from two directions. Metalwork was an important part of the life of the English colonies and blacksmiths were of high value in the isolation of colonial living. They learned to fabricate elegant architectural embellishments, as well as the instruments of everyday life when the great Colonial and Federal houses arose in Georgian influenced New England. But the most exuberant ironwork in American architectural life came not so much from the east, but rather up from the South. New Orleans. Ironwork has always been one of the amazing signature characteristics of New Orleans architectural artistry. The abundance of ironwork balconies, railings, gates, and highly decorative filigree trim created a unique genre of local expression and was the making of domestic architecture in New Orleans. Influenced by the city's crossroads European colonial roots at the strategic juncture of the most important gulf port, this style is expressive of the influence of both French Empire and English Regency styles. In the highly ornate French Quarter, time stands still and evokes a beauty and craftsmanship that continues, even in the present, to be an enduring art form.

Iron ornamentation in the United States flourished in the 19th century. Iron was the flower of American industrialization and it was ennobled in the construction of such signature American landmarks as the Brooklyn Bridge and the Flat Iron Building in New York. The firm of J. W. Fiske and Company became one the nation's most well known and sought after manufacturers of ironwork design and their distinguished metalwork added a distinctive beauty to the character of New York. Ironwork became a popular end-of-the-century hallmark as a resurgence of revivalist styles of architectural styles incorporated its decoration into their design. Queen Anne architecture, for instance, in the 1880s, is notable for its characteristic iron porches, balconies, and ornate porch rails. Even the fresh designs of the Chicago School, exemplified by the work of Louis Sullivan and Daniel Burnham, made use of extraordinary elements of ornamental ironwork decoration in the stunning and inventive prototypes of their modern American skyscraper styles. There followed a growing interest in their iron screens, fancy elevator grates, highly effusive scroll staircases, and grates in elaborate flowing flowery designs of intricate organic ironwork. All of which framed some of the most singular and exciting architecture in America.

Modern American cities underwent growth spurts in the late 19th century. In many cities, the federal government undertook the construction of courthouses and office buildings that all seemed to reflect the grandeur of the national spirit. Often built in revivalist styles, these stately edifices utilized not only the latest inventions, such as electricity and the elevator, but also extensive ironwork ornamentation that expressed the national identity in heroic and patriotic symbols made of iron. At the same time, a new sensitivity to public safety in tall buildings led to the construction of iron fire escapes in large numbers. They too came to reflect the discriminating fashion of the popular tastes of the day. By the turn of the century America saw its urban landscape altered forever by the technology, power, and beauty of iron.

In France, Alexander Eiffel built his timeless monument to French industrialization with his tower for the Paris Exposition, and later constructed an elaborate two-tiered iron bridge over the River Douro in the Portuguese city of Porto which remains today a startling monument to iron design. Imbued with the distinctive influence of the Art Nouveau movement, the French embraced the use of decorative ironwork. It lent itself well to the organic shapes and contours of this style. Even the familiar rust color, so valued by Nouveau artists, was living reality of cast ironwork. It was without equal as a significant material for avant-garde design in Le Belle Époque.

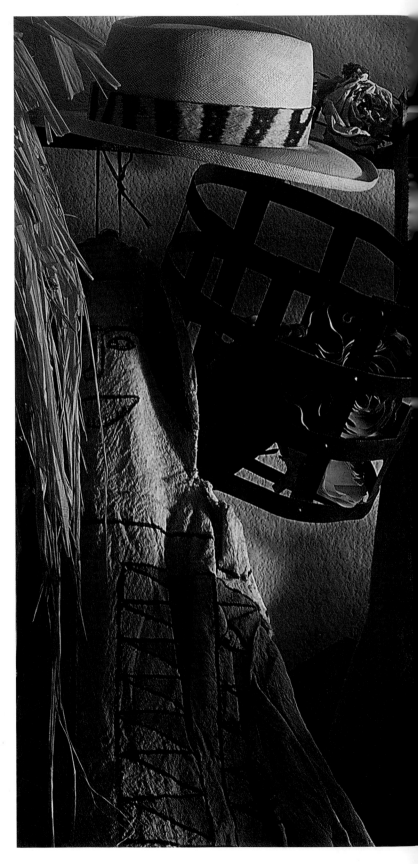

Left: A sturdy but whimsical closet of cast iron and wrought iron decorative embellishments. The heavy duty coat rack is American cast iron. Decorative pieces are wrought iron: the trumpeting angel in flight, the ornamental iron cage, and the dungeon like basket for closet collectables.

Garden Items, Fountains, and Furniture

Be fruitful, and multiply, and replenish the earth.

Genesis 1:28

Above: An urn of carved Scottish limestone has a delicate symmetry and hearty elegance filled with dwarf banana tree and wild curry plants.

Right: This superb French arbor in a suburban Chicago garden looks very Parisian with classic French park table and chairs and gravel path. The sculpture of Aphrodite adds a splendid air of exotic refinement in this very private domestic landscape.

Below: "The Fountain of the Pleasant Rabbits," by Howard Van Doren Shaw, circa 1920. This delightful device of delicately carved Illinois limestone has a motif of carrots and rabbits and was original to the Shaw mansion in Lake Forest, Illinois. The present owners, however, uncovered it while landscaping their garden where it had been buried and forgotten for decades by the previous owners. Now restored and returned to its central front drive location, it represents one of Shaw's most noble works.

Gardens come in all shapes and sizes. They can roll for acres swept by ocean winds, wild and unpredictable, or they can stand tight and contained filling the window boxes and patio trellis of a Manhattan vintage high-rise. They can be low budget or high maintenance. But as any real garden lover knows, big or small they are extensions of the gardener's larger world.

In Europe, over the centuries the sense of connection with nature gave rise to a deep harmony between house and garden and formed gardens to be intimate components of domestic life. Gardens historically have been the domain of the wealthy and European gardens, particularly in England, were classically designed by the 18th century, laid out by the finest architects of the day to complement the great country houses. Fueled by massive fortunes, remarkable architects such as Sir William Chambers and garden designers such as Capability Brown laid out great gardens filled with the vestiges of classical antiquity. In the 18th century gardens were thick with Greek and Roman temples, Chinese pagodas, elaborate follies, and great fountains. Such ornamental architecture added to the grandeur of country estates and lured the inhabitants of the house outdoors in good weather. Because they were natural extensions of great homes, garden ornaments reflected the same ostentation. Finials and obelisks, geometric pediments, and balustrades brought the flavor of the house to the garden.

Grand views and scenic panoramas were enjoyed from stone garden benches detailed with classical embellishments. Imposing curved semicircular seats resembling benches used in the Roman senate became popular in the later Regency period. Classical detailing flowed through the whole gamut of garden objects, reinforcing the restrained glory of ancient epochs. Sundials sat upon plinths that echoed Rome and birdbaths perched upon balusters reminiscent of Ancient Greece. In garden niches the gods of ancient civilizations and mythological deities looked out upon enchanted landscapes.

To 18th century sensibilities, such splendor rivaled what they perceived to be the romance and nobility of the past. They reclined in nature and strolled over textured lawns with sunlit temples rising in their views. Architectural follies and temples of the winds, such as those designed by Vanbrugh as at Castle Howard in Yorkshire and by James Stewart at Mt. Stewart House in Newtownards in Ireland, transformed people's ordinary sense of reality. Their spires, domes, and columns reshaped the horizon. Garden ornamentation was not merely "outdoor furniture," it was a means by which nature was engaged and caressed. Like the nobles of ancient Rome, they wandered in classical ascendancy like gods themselves with nature displayed in excess tranquility before their gaze.

The power and effect of such gardens engendered a unique intensity within English culture that continues in the present. It established gardens as a demonstrable expression of a broader

Above: This elegant hand carved wooden artifact comes from a temple in Thailand and adds an air of the exotic to this outdoor setting. Asian artifacts are a remarkable addition to any interior and bring a sense of the folk tradition of craftsmanship as well as timelessness in artistry.

Right: A 19th century fountain and 20th century reflecting pool designed by David Adler, circa 1926. With carved 19th century limestone Putti set in the thick of nature, it demonstrates Adler's abiding love for the classical motif, as well as the refined linear designs of its simplicity.

Left: This remarkable garden in a Chicago Gold Coast courtyard mixes high styles and eclectic textures. The Neo-classical urns atop the central niche reflect the overall design of the house. Art Deco touches come with the evocative staircase and tall garden sculpture by Jordan Masur in sea horse motif; the fountain in the background is complemented by the reflecting pool and lower fountain with bronze mythological figure. Two ancient sphinxes, a very French addition, add to the artistry of the architectural feeling. Cast iron urns are brimming with flowers and complete the richness of this urban paradise.

cultural identity and national pride. This understanding later led to the establishment of more public gardens to which the wider populace would have access. Nature's transforming influence had a deep significance. The impact of public gardens would have an effect on all.

Popular tastes had a significant influence upon garden ornamentation throughout the 19th century. In England, the expanding world of the Victorians and the effects of their global colonial expansion stimulated popular interest in the exotic lands with which they grew more familiar. In gardens, new horticultural discoveries in the foreign reaches of the globe were popularized. Scientific interests helped establish many new garden bloom varieties such as azaleas and rhododendrons. Imports from Asia led to

interest in many cultural adaptations of Oriental fashions and styles. Nowhere was this more significant than in gardens where the influence of Chinese designs brought exciting elements into garden life. Victorians were enchanted with the items such as Chinese trellises, stone lanterns, and Chinoiserie gates.

In the 19th century, the medieval ruins even served as garden ornamentation. At Tresco Abbey, on the Isles of Scilly, off England's Cornish coast, Augustus Smith, the Lord Proprietor of the Isles, established an extraordinary tropical garden within the ruins, taking advantage of the sub-tropical climate there. His plantings came from across the globe and flourished in Gulf Stream breezes. It is said that the extraordinary varieties of daffodils there were left

Left: These four white French metal garden chairs, circa 1950s, portray a kitschy modern character that is both fanciful and delicate. The wire legs and the sun burst geometry of the seat and back convey a kind of Riviera swagger.

Below left: This wrought iron Gothic Revival garden bench, with a remarkably distressed patina, sits beneath Illinois's oldest elm tree in this lavish Lake Forest, Illinois, garden. Beds of blue bells encircle this rather monastic styled garden settee.

Right: This urban garden patio looks more like Southern California in the 1960s than downtown Chicago, but this remarkable outpost unfolds an extraordinary collection of timeless "flower power" style. The deep orange color is a hallmark of the period's design.

by long departed monks. The garden still survives today, its Gothic character a dramatic reminder of Victorian passions.

But perhaps the most lasting contribution of the Victorian age to the elements of garden life was the introduction of cast iron as a fashionable material for garden ornamentation. The stone embellishments of the previous generation soon gave way to more durable and affordable manufactured items for garden use. As cities expanded and towns grew into larger urban communities, the new middle class utilized the product of their industrial age to ornament their more modest gardens. Cast iron tables and chairs provided a most reliable product for garden use. Even in more elaborate country gardens, cast iron was more easily obtained, thanks to the benefits of mass manufacturing, than the costly handmade stone items of past. Fountains fabricated from cast iron were soon used in both private and public gardens. Cast iron also provided the Victorians with a material that lent itself to the extravagant ornate excess in design for which stone was a more limited medium. It permitted a wide variety of decorative styles such as horticultural motifs, and because it was less expensive than the costly items of the past, more people could invest in garden ornamentation and garden art. Cast iron birdbaths, urns, and finials dotted garden landscapes.

During the Victorian age, many great country houses established "glasshouses," or hothouses, in which climatic conditions could be controlled and more readily support delicate varieties of plants. Palms and ferns were particularly popular as were other fragile botanicals such as citrus fruits. Many people became enamored with the concept of glasshouses

Garden Items, Fountains, and Furniture

Left: This tapering Tuscan column adds a heavy touch of Roman antiquity to this garden court and is complemented by the decorative artifact of the regal equine head. The waters of this pool have an ancient feel to them.

Right: These figures depict the musical life of the ancient world and add a mystical artistry to this planter thick with floral growth.

following the Great Exhibition in London of 1855. Glasshouses evolved in many country homes into extensions of garden life, cast iron furniture permitted dining and socializing in the exotic indoor solarium. Palm courts would become a staple of Victorian refinement.

Fountains also became a staple of garden ornamentation. Whether they were mounted on a garden wall or occupied a central position, fountains, more than any other piece of garden ornament, sought to delight the viewer. They cooled and refreshed, relaxing the spirit and quieting the soul. Fountains encapsulated the aesthetics of garden romanticism. In garden use, fountains became charming spectacles, both restful and visually pleasing, while providing an opportunity for the introduction of unique architectural sculpture and design. Classical, Renaissance, and wide revivalist styles flourished in the music and grace of fountains.

The technological development of the 19th century, as in so many aspects of life, reshaped the gardens of the era—popular styles became easily available and permitted the replication of previously hard to obtain items. Everything from statuary to garden gnomes were plentiful and affordable.

The rigors and character of American's colonial beginnings had little room for the extravagancies of garden luxuries such as those back in England. American 18th century gardens were far more likely to contain vegetables and fruits than the horticultural ornamentation of aristocratic English tastes. There was a built-in practicality in American gardens, a colonial utility. Even in

Left: This outstanding garden pergola is thick with abundant whisteria and provides a romantic vista rich with delicate growths at the start of summer. Cast iron urns brimming with exotic growths complement the uncontrolled movement of nature.

Right: The iron wheel of a rough timbered cart adds an old world flavor to this garden rich in the harvest of sunflowers. A decidedly Provencal touch graces this lush gardenscape.

the more lavish private decorative colonial gardens there was a tendency to utilize whatever was near at hand to fashion decorative ornaments. Wood was a standard and plentiful material in everyday life and was implemented easily in garden use instead of costly and difficult to acquire stone. Americans also had weather constraints to contend with in the development of garden design.

However, there were exceptions. No garden in America was more elegant and refined than that of Thomas Jefferson at Monticello. In the Virginia countryside he fashioned gardens reflective of classical antiquity, replete with the structural influences popular in European tastes for classical inspired architecture. But he also demonstrated the new Republic's passion for utility and practicality. Jefferson merged the ideals of classical antiquity with rugged American idealism. His garden was fashioned not just for beauty, but also as a working center of American botanical inventiveness. His efforts are visible still in the garden's exuberant timelessness.

Jefferson's restrained enlightenment and gentleman gardener character did not remain the dominant influence in America garden ornamentation though. Americans, with little practical experience of private decorative gardening, turned to Europe for inspiration and many began to import European statuary, armillary spheres, sundials, garden furniture, fencing, finials, urns, and other decorative embellishments along with designs from European garden architects. It was not until late in 19th century, when industrial success produced barons of wide commercial empires, that the direction and influence in American gardens began to change.

There was an exciting sense of American pragmatism at work during the boom days of industrialization that seemed to invigorate American attitudes. As inventiveness swept the land, American tastes became more accepting of new all-American styles. Gardeners were pioneering a pragmatic sense of taste in decorative garden design and cast iron quickly became a great influence on popular garden fashions. Copies of a wide assortment of architectural styles were easily and cheaply produced, helping to reinforce a hearty American eclecticism that never has gone out of style. American tastes continue to be practical, influenced significantly by the twin forces of climate and geography. Successful American gardens, and hence garden ornamentation, would come to respect and reflect these unbendable dimensions of nature. Because America as a nation is so large, with wide

variance in temperature zones and growing seasons, American gardens express a dramatic variety in botanical and ornamental styles. A strong sense of regional style underscores the American passion for gardens and garden ornament.

Domestic gardens developed a decidedly social dimension in American life. Americans relished the opportunity to be out in nature, even if that meant a simple urban backyard. By the early decades of the 20th century a considerable expansion took place in the manufacture and design of comfortable, functional, and attractive garden furniture. It was at this time that the ever-popular spring steel chair became fashionable. First created in France, it was an American staple by the 1920s. American gardens bloomed with wire chairs, wrought iron tables and chairs, glass top cocktail tables, wire carts, wrought steel benches, wicker furniture, wooden Adirondack suites, and hickory bark tables and chairs. America was producing both wide variety and high quality in an ever expanding garden furniture trade.

Gardens have never been more popular in American culture than they are in our own time. Garden enthusiasts have a significant network of resources with which to acquire both the skills and elements necessary for designing and implementing great gardens. Nowhere is this more true than in America's cities where an ever-growing younger population has rediscovered a strong sense of garden aesthetics. Urban gardeners have the income and the time to create environments of beauty and style. This means that garden ornamentation has never been more valued. In addition to the traditional components of garden decorative design—birdbaths, sundials, statues, urns, putti, cherubs, sphinx, and the like, trends are appearing in which gardeners utilize a wide variety of architectural elements. The prerequisites are for quality, authenticity, and patina. Chunks of architectural material—capstones, keystones, capitals, roundels, and pediments—give gardens a stately and a historic embellishment not that far removed from the aesthetics of grand 18th century perceptions. People want a good view, an elegant panorama, even if it is just a tiny scape. With the wide opportunity of obtaining salvaged architectural elements, gardeners have a wide array of ornaments with which to give dignity and a sense of beauty to contemporary garden design. The possibilities are limitless.

Far Left: Mid-19th century French cast iron convent bed with brass finials sits outside in a small area of a garden. Mattress ticking and pillows can adorn it on sunny days serving as a splendid couch. With the addition of a small board to fit the frame, the bed becomes a plant holder thick with pots and urns.

Left: A tableau of garden furniture. An interesting collection of distressed white French garden furniture from the 1940s, including serving table, drink cart, table, chairs, bird cage, and an herb planter with carrier. In the background stand a pair of one-sided white wood columns. An 1880s church pew from Savannah Georgia sits beneath four Welsh leaded Edwardian style casement windows. Ever watchful is the zinc cast iron golden retriever with crystal collar. An oversized French ceramic teapot adds a Wonderland quality to this quirky setting amid the finials and corbels.

Commercial and Industrial Salvage

And did the Countenance Divine
Shine forth upon our clouded hills?
And was the Jerusalem builded here
Among these dark Satanic mills?

William Blake

Above: Gas sign from a 1940s gas station found in Salvage One, Chicago. Inexpensive pieces like this, either restored or left in an authentically distressed state, make a refreshing change from framed prints on any wall in the home.

Right: Classic 1950s American neon motel sign used as wall sculpture in a passageway between garage and kitchen in a reconfigured commercial trucking garage, now converted into a domestic residence. The neon light reflects in the polished enamel finish of the home's white tiles beside the window overlooking the garden.

Below: Turn-of-the century Parisian storefront clock with roman numerals and Arabic inner numerals that create a 24 hour timepiece. Such public timepieces were an integral part of everyday life, as many individuals did not have the luxury of personal watches. Businesses rendered a great public service by utilizing clocks in busy shopping areas. Oversized timepieces lend themselves well to many innovative domestic interiors.

Commercial salvage is the material and equipment of restaurants and businesses. Industrial salvage is the material and equipment of factories and manufacturing plants. Commercial is small and practical in its scale. Industrial is burly and technical.

It is no secret that there have been huge shifts in the industrial manufacturing base in the United States in the past twenty-five years. There was a time when the economy of the nation rested with what appeared to be an endless source of cheap labor and national determinism. In truth, such was the story of America from the very beginning. The original thirteen colonials were themselves developed for such purpose. But the nation has now shifted from a manufacturing economic base to a service based economy. More and more, American manufacturing is something that is farmed out to other nations. Our shirts are made in Thailand, our shoes in Portugal, our cell phones in China, and our cars in Mexico. The economic reasoning of the past three decades has discovered that it is cheaper and more productive to shift our manufacturing elsewhere. Just look at the label inside your Nikes.

The result has brought about the closure of many small and large manufacturing plants around the country. This is really nothing new. As technologies were reinvented continuously since the start of the Industrial Revolution to the present, someone is always making machinery and equipment obsolete. It is the same today in the passage to the computer and high tech industries. All of this leads in one way or another to the abundance of commercial and industrial salvage.

As manufacturing plants and factories shut down, beyond the immediate economic realities involved is another reality—the availability of many specialty items of equipment and elements of architectural design. Industrial lighting is just one element that has high reuse. Imagine the scale of a factory or plant, the acres and acres of space all needing illumination. Usually this meant state of the art fixtures. Lots and lots of fixtures. This is equipment that can be used with great success in other environments. Industrial lighting is a very popular commodity, especially sought after by those who are living in the flip side of the downturn in manufacturing—industrial loft dwellers.

With the loss of significant manufacturing, the industrial buildings in which they were located become vacant. In older American cities, such areas of manufacturing were usually located just outside the city centers. Today this means prime location. Changes in urban demographics make neighborhoods like this more desirable than ever as they are usually conveniently located with quick access to city centers. Many American cities are experiencing the change in use of many buildings from industrial and commercial to residential. It is changing the ways cities live and shifting large

Right: Signage predominates in this handsome kitchen with horizontal pine plank walls. Carnival game wheels and cola display advertising add a complementary touch. Sign and form are important and bring a sense of unity to both the eating area and the kitchen space.

Far Right: 20th century American signage: a hand-painted life-size nurse executed on wooden board used for a blood drive campaign. The use of such visuals was a common part of the American way of life and demonstrated both a purposeful design as well as important element of folk art. The wind swept appearance of the nurse adds to the drama and importance of the cause.

populations, creating residential communities in imaginative locations. As these environments are redesigned, they are generating big interest in industrial salvage. Ironically, they are also helping to create it. New urban residential spaces offer a wider set of possibilities in creating inspired and practical interior spaces. When your living space is one gigantic space, often without conventional features such as walls, the possibilities are endless. A very different set of design needs are created. Scale and proportion changes. These are not places for little love seats and frilly curtains. Large industrial spaces require large solutions to their specialized questions of interior design and the appropriate use of space. After all, the urban pioneers for whom such stark spaces and altered domestic interiors are home are most likely themselves design renegades. The texture and utilitarian character of industrial design elements lend themselves well to the height and width of this new style of urban living.

Commercial salvage is another rich reservoir of functional, reusable, alternate use materials found in salvage centers today. This is the collected treasure of butcher shops, Chinese restaurants, hat shops, ice cream parlors, candy stores, department stores, bars, saloons, hotels, eye doctor offices, toy stores, theaters, banks, jewelry stores, bakeries, schools, churches, zoos, motels, photography studios, convents, monasteries, and dress shops.

What emerges is a unique collection of scales, weights, and measures, display and advertising objects, like faux meats and vegetables, pagoda

booths, hat forms, tables and chairs, cash registers, candy jars, mannequins, bars, juke boxes, swivel stools, mail slots, key racks, theater seats, movie projectors, ticket booths, safes, safety deposit boxes, teller cages, display cases, pie racks, baking pans, desks, blackboards, pews, candles sticks, votive light racks, kneelers, fish tanks, bird cages, beds, coffee shop counters, towels dispensers, developing trays, dress racks, hat boxes, mirrors, refectory tables, sewing tables, sundials, clocks, and signage.

Commercial salvage joins industrial salvage as a practical resource for large scale and unusual materials that might not fit the neat trends of domestic America, but are popular because they complement the scale of oversized urban interiors.

The popular use of commercial and industrial salvage today in domestic interiors validates a long held belief about the artistic excellence and design significance involved in the creation and fabrication of materials for America's business. Often, even the most technical piece of machinery or industrial equipment was fashioned with a high level of precision and craftsmanship. It was not good business to create machines or devices that could not stand the test of time or stress. Industrial equipment often followed a standard of excellence in craftsmanship that has long since deteriorated in other manufactured American goods and products. The culture of American business bred machines that were not only capable of performing the task for which they were created, but often with an eye to elements of beauty as well as function. Many used the finest materials available—the best metals, the costliest alloys, the best formed glass, and the most modern shapes and geometric proportions. Industrial equipment has often been compared to the linear and geometric symmetrical proportion of Neo-classical design. Amid the drafting, calculations, and countless applications of wheels and arms and chains, belts, pulleys, and bobbins, machines arose from the imaginative mind of man. They retain an objective beauty in their form. Many retain a full or partial component of their utility and use.

Above left: Contemporary American office desk and chair fashioned entirely from salvage. The desk was made from a heavily rusted heating furnace with exhaust vent at front. The desk light, also fashioned from salvage, is connected to the desk. A handsome red leather and chrome, hand stitched American barber chair, circa late 1960s, complements the overall design scheme.

Left: These Parisian enamel commercial clock face panels of Roman numerals, circa late-19th century, show high craftsmanship and rich detail. Though no clockwork mechanism accompanies these panels, they present optimum opportunity for use in interior settings. Enameling is a prized artistic endeavor and easily adds character to any environment.

Right: Painted wood and copper Roman numeral clock face with zodiac/astrological motif, circa 1900, formerly in the tower of Schlitz Brewery in Milwaukee, Wisconsin. Today it is housed in a fashionable Chicago Italian bistro. The numerals have a German Gothic quality to them, which would be apropos of their original location. The piece was obtained through a local salvage purveyor.

Left: Two views of vintage American signage: below are 20th century American hand painted panels of three female portraits from a 1940s era beauty shop advertisement. Above, late-19th century American peddler wagon's side panel advertising the wide variety of assorted wares carried in the wagon.

Above right: Classic American bulb signage from Chicago's Avenue Motel. The six-foot letters are metal and are emblematic of a lost piece of America road travel that was so popular in the 1950s and 1960s. In some ways they were the banners of small town America and the tacky reflection of big-city life.

Below right: Glazed terra cotta letters from the front of a 1920s Chicago building. Terra cotta was a popular finishing feature of many American commercial buildings, such as small office blocks or banks.

For instance, 19th century Victorian industry was thick with assorted mills and textile companies both in American and Britain. They required very specialized equipment then, later adapting to more modern times. As such businesses closed or further adapted, a large supply of very curious machines and equipment often went on the auction block. Great wooden drums for pressing fabric and huge spools for winding thread are just some of the types of industrial elements found. Their adaptation to contemporary usage is limitless. Perhaps a dozen ninety-five year old sewing machines do not seem like such an advantageous auction purchase. Think again. Each one comes with its own wooden cabinet and a long list of secondary practical uses.

Factories, particularly before World War I, operated on low scale assembly line piece work. Workers, often women, spent hours sitting at very long tables, engaged in any number of handwork projects. These tables are an extremely valuable commodity today. Such factory tables often have heavy hardwood construction and character rich distressed finishes. Because they needed to fit many workers around them, they come in unusually long lengths. Such tables make outstanding additions in modern homes.

Industrial lighting is another major element of high value in salvage centers today. Advances in lighting technology, particularly since World War II, brought innovative and enhanced systems. Factories normally utilized large numbers of fixtures in proportion with their size. Consequently, sup-

plies of good exterior and interior lighting are now available. Individual fixtures, made with top-of-the-line design, provide efficient technologically advanced apparatus, often of high quality materials that add a taste of industrial chic to any living environment. Industrial design is a powerful and effective contrast to other, more historically expressive ornamentation, such as Rococo or Art Nouveau.

Commercial salvage offers a wide variety of curious and effective components for adaptation in contemporary interiors. Like elements of industrial design, commercial products too were often fashioned with a high degree of artistic quality and merit. Many items were used in very specialized and technical types of business. Many enterprises by their nature require specialized equipment: for instance, the medical profession or barber shops. There is no end of finely crafted chairs and tables that make their way into salvage centers from these professions. Barber chairs, particularly vintage chairs, are the Cadillac of vintage design. Today, they may be formed from plastic and cheap metals, but in the old days they were heavy duty chrome. They had porcelain arm rests and studded fine leather seats and backs. Hand pump hydraulics made them highly functional as well as handsome. A vintage barber chair today is as artistically fashionable as a Corvette.

Some more macabre businesses, like funeral homes, are an endless source of vintage curiosities. What about a turn of the century embalming

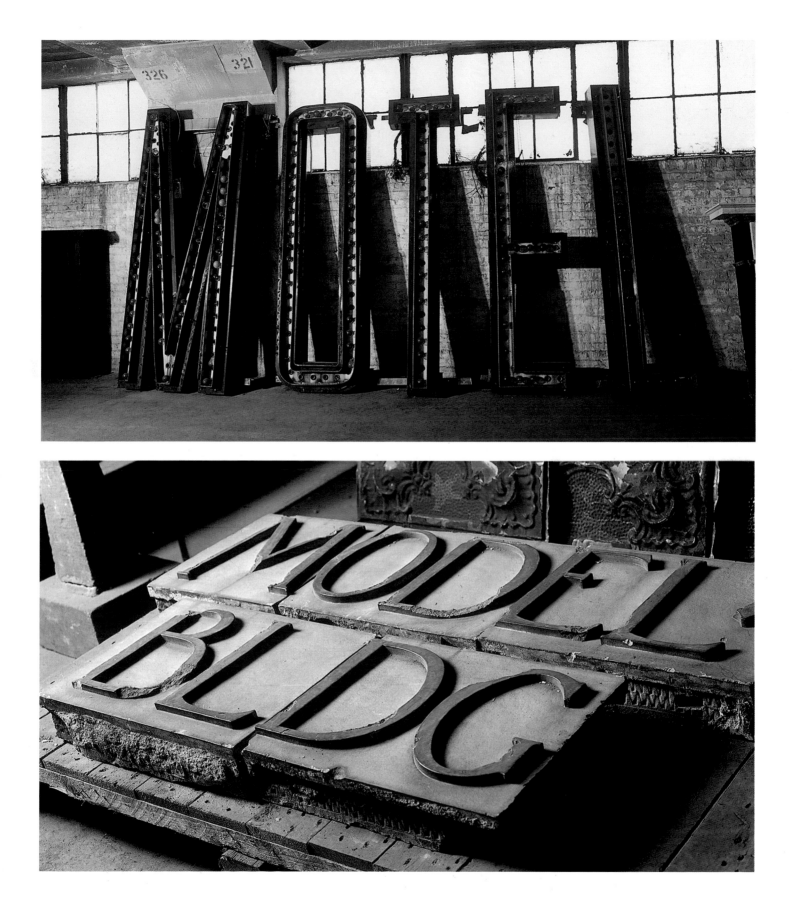

Left: A glazed porcelain figure or mannequin with the upper body shape of a woman and the bottom wooden slats for display purposes. It makes a markedly balanced complement to the interior of this room whose rough horizontal wall planking and exposed rafters (reflected in the mirror) connote an American Victorian design format.

Right: An unusual display of hand forms used in the making of gloves. The forms have a strange but intriguing sculptural beauty to them, particularly arranged on this tabletop in front of an outstanding beveled window. Tools of the glove-making trade appear to rest on the table as well.

table? They are available and highly functional, though you probably need to refer to it as a "lab table" if you want anyone to eat off it.

With shifting populations in many American cities, many city churches once built for teaming throngs of immigrants, now no longer serve the same needs. Many city parish churches have closed in the past decade and their contents sold. A wide variety of ecclesiastical furnishings often become available. For instance, church pews are a very prized commodity. They are usually beautifully carved and very practical, for they make serving large groups convenient. Placing two pews on either side of a long factory table is a remarkable blending of two very complementary styles. Smaller pews, the two or three seat model, are very popular in front halls and on stairway landings. They can be cushioned and make a fine addition in the home. Pews with a decidedly ornate Gothic ornamentation are particularly prized.

Schools are another source of practical items of salvage. Desks of a wide variety of styles, no longer considered practical in modern classrooms, frequently find their way into salvage centers. Even desks with a foreign pedigree can be found. French wooden school desks have a remarkable quality to them and are aesthetically pleasing. School lockers are very practical items that can be used effectively in many interiors. In a wide open space such as a loft, a whole wall of lockers can become both a practical and artistic enhancement. The lockers are perfect for stowing clutter, coats, cleaning supplies, brooms, mops, even dishware, towels, and umbrellas. If they have interesting patinas they can be an object of art themselves.

Businesses are the most significant generators of advertising signage. An entire culture has grown up around the vintage artistry of advertising design and the construction of public advertising, and today signs are a very popular element of commercial salvage. Whether they are from butcher shops, motels, gas stations, pubs, or clothing stores, signage is both a craft and an art. Signs can be used effectively in many interiors. They are highly figurative, evocative of special eras, and for many are nostalgic reminders of special moments in life. The imagery and artistry of signage has a unique potential for interior ornamentation. In eclectic environments signs are often the anchor of room design. For instance, a large plywood ham, a six foot hot dog, or a dramatic painted angel can add a fluid artistry to an interior that goes far beyond the message of the advertisement. Focus on the quality of the artistry and the beauty of its design.

Commercial and industrial salvage have altered the market place and rearranged the interiors of contemporary homes. A growing popular taste demonstrates a large shift in popular fashion. Fifty years ago, few domestic interiors would have appreciated the introduction

Left: The textile industry of Victorian England is reflected in this barrel-shaped hollow pieced-wood canister drum from a Midlands factory, circa 1880s, which could, for instance, be used as a really unusual planter. In the foreground is a primitive turn of the century dentist's chair of wrought iron with adjustable seat.

Right: American black leather and white porcelain trimmed swivel barber's chair, circa 1910, with original brass tacking on the upholstery and chrome foot pedals and trim, plus hand pump to lower and raise the height of chair. In the background is a set of 1920s French school metal lockers with original blue distressed patina.

of shop or factory fixtures. In that era, standards of design had a more limited, conventional approach. The lines of division between commercial design and residential design were very clear. During the previous five decades from the turn of the century to the decade following World War II, millions of individuals moved from the ranks of the newly arrived immigrant to full fledged middle class Americans and cherished middle class standards and sensibilities. The 1950s were the apex of that constrained, repressive era. Within a decade, the 1960s, a powerful transforming cultural movement, would alter forever the narrow standards and tastes of the past. Out of this experience, nothing would ever be the same. This has been especially true in the arts.

No suburban mom, no urban society matron for that matter, could conceivably imagine using industrial lighting in their home back then, or include the addition of a large piece of signage to their matching living room suite of furniture.

Now, however, an endless array of interesting and creative items formerly used in commercial or industrial enterprises are changing the face of domestic interiors through their eclectic blend and mixing with other design styles. In the mix, a remarkable and very personal design form is shaped. It underscores the creative potential hidden within these treasures' artistry and timeless design.

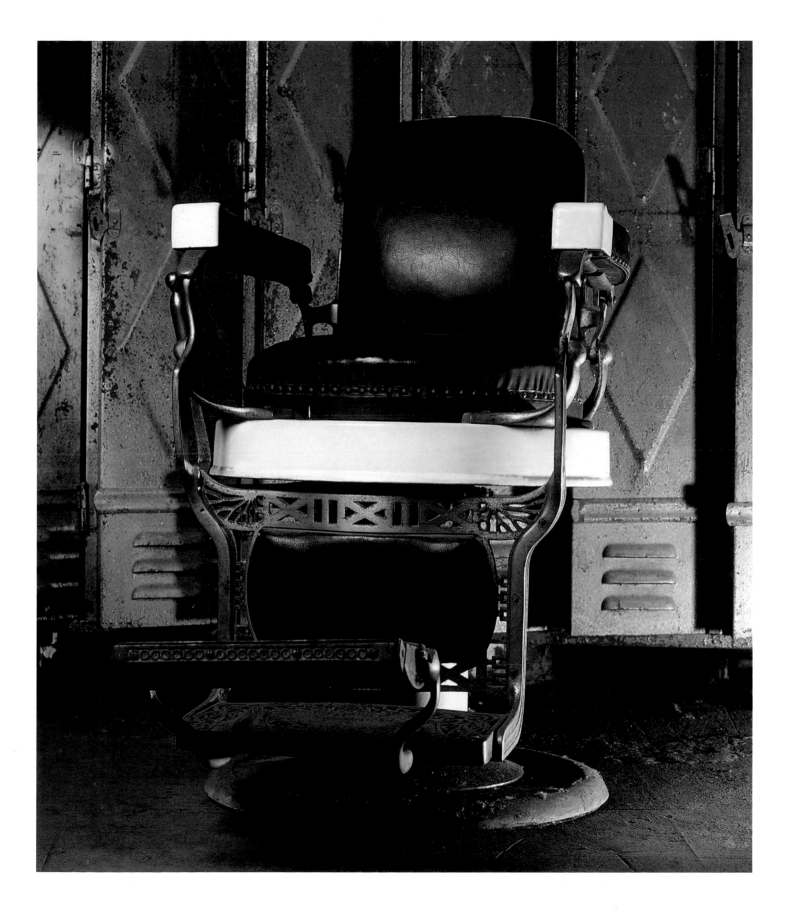

Ornamental Stonework and Ecclesiastical Ornamentation

He builded better than he knew:
The conscious stone to beauty grew.

Ralph Waldo Emerson

Above: Carved limestone bull's head, circa 1890, from the Detroit Eastern Market, home of the Motor City's wholesale meat industry.

Right: Tableau containing: (foreground left) a terra cotta fragment by George Elmslie in the Prairie School style and (center) a large pair of terra cotta finials with acanthus leaf motif from the Presidential Hotel, Kansas City, Missouri.

Below: Two sphinxes frame a garden walk in this Lake Forest, Illinois, estate. Egyptian themed artifacts appeared in abundance in France following Napolean's conquering of Egypt in the first decade of the 19th century. Such luxurious pieces remain wildly popular.

At Castletown House, near Dublin, Thomas Conolly, the Speaker of the Irish Parliament built the finest palladian house in Ireland in 1722. Its classical detail is overwhelming. But nothing captures the attention of visitors more than a visit on a rainy day. For no matter how heavy the rain beats against the house, its stone façade never changes color. Its unique Ardbracken stone retains the same patina in sunshine or in wet shadow. Regretfully, in the almost three centuries since its construction, no one has yet located the mysterious quarry from which this stone was cut.

Stone has been an important material for architects since the dawn of time. Or at least since man left the hut, the lean-to, or the cave. Stone is the ultimate material for building. Rugged, durable, and surprisingly pliable, in more modern times, it has been responsible for more buildings of style and grace than any other material. When the architectural principals of ancient Greece and Rome were rediscovered by Neo-classical architects and craftsmen in the 18th century, they translated the symmetry and proportionality of its restrained form best in stone. In England, none served the purpose better than Portland Stone, a remarkable substance made famous by the best architects of the day. In this stone the great buildings of the day rose for domestic, ecclesiastical, and governmental use.

In the 19th century, the Victorians found in stone a worthy material, which they would use to revive the architectural style and ornament of the Middle Ages as Gothic Revival flourished in popular tastes. It was also the proper substance for the new age of monument construction by which the Victorians paid homage to their military and cultural achievements. With stone they brought back the age of gargoyles, flying buttresses, tracery window carvings, hooded window moldings, vaulted ceilings, clerestory windows, oriel windows, and countless medieval-inspired spires dotted the land. Stone ornament with a decidedly royal persona, such as the familiar crowned lion symbolizing the royal nature of the constitutional monarchy, decorated the House of Parliament. And countless stone insignia expressing the nation's regal nature and prestige decorated endless public buildings, façades, and government centers. Stone helped to recreate the heroic myth of Britain's ancient Gothic past at an important time in its history.

The Gothic Revival in America was a decidedly less regal, but no less romantic era. The elaborate palaces designed in this style on the other side of the Atlantic were fashioned for a different kind of royalty – industrial royalty. People who had made their fortunes in the markets of the boom in American finance and the personal fortunes made through coal and steel and railroads and gold. The kings of those industries found stone an appropriate material with which to fashion monuments to both their success and their generosity. Many 19th century American entrepreneurs built elaborate palaces for themselves. In Chicago, hotel impresario Potter Palmer engaged Henry Ives Cobb to construct a castle for his wife Bertha on the shores of Lake Michigan for almost

Left: Dramatically regal limestone heads from Chicago's Broadway Strand Theater. The theater was pulled down long ago, but these kingly heads have more life left in them and have great possibility.

Right: Aggregate bas relief sculpture panel of athletes in the Art Deco style from the façade of the original Chicago Stadium designed by Hall Lawrence Ratcliff. The stadium was long the home of the Chicago Blackhawks and the Chicago Bulls, and also saw numerous national presidential conventions.

two million dollars—hundreds of millions in today's adjusted currency. Beneath its castellated towers the Palmers ate off gold dishes and collected French Impressionist paintings. When John D. Rockefeller endowed the University of Chicago to fashion an ivy-league outpost in the Midwest, its buildings rose in Gothic splendor, gargoyled, parapeted, and arched like something behind an Oxford wall. The power of its architecture said it all. This institution would be connected to an intellectual tradition that was ageless and tied to the great European style of education.

The stone of Gothic Revival ornamentation became familiar on many fancy university and college campuses. But what really expanded the use of this architectural style in the United States was the extraordinary building boom in ecclesiastical architecture that came in the last decades of the 19th century. The largest example stood on New York's Fifth Avenue—St. Patrick's Cathedral. It was the spiritual home to countless Irish who saw in its medieval splendor and majesty a new source of pride as they drove the streetcar or pounded the beat. Ecclesiastical architecture had a profound affect on the church faithful. Across the nation countless other Gothic churches rose, fed by the nickel and dimes of uncountable immigrants and the generosity of those who found their fortunes. Gothic design triggered a sentimental response within the believing population. It carried a soothing monastic tranquility. Its sight lines

and architectural perspective lifted people's vision and pointed toward heaven. In America, Gothic Revival was soon synonymous with ecclesiastical design.

Pews, elaborate chairs, furniture, windows, altars, communion rails, pulpits, statue niches, down spouts, gutters, lamps, chandeliers, candlesticks, candelabra, chalices, and canopied cathedral thrones mirrored the romanticized fashions of the Middle Ages and created a familiar and popular religious style among many Americans. Ecclesiastical architecture in America differed from the European in that everything in America was new. It was reinvented and revived. But the overall affect was still the same.

Today, it is not difficult to uncover elements of both stone ornamentation and ecclesiastical design. While stone is durable, it is not indestructible and even in the great cathedrals of Europe, stonework is in need of constant repair. Often pediments, corbels, decorative faces, and other items are removed and these items often find their way into salvage yards or auction markets. In American cities, particularly in the inner cities, change and demographic shifts sometimes result in church closures. This in turn results in articles and elements of ecclesiastical design again finding their way into salvage markets. All these items lend themselves well to new use in domestic interiors. Exercising the design creed of the Victorians, everything will work inside your home.

Left: Hand carved limestone grotesque fountainhead. The open mouth permits water to flow through the stone and flow into a pond or a fountain. This handsome head measures two feet by three feet.

Right: A terra cotta griffin, circa 1920, from a public building in St. Louis, Missouri. This mythic beast was described as having the wings and head of an eagle and the body of a lion.

Ornamentation reached a new and thoroughly modern expression in America in the architecture that came from the Chicago School in the last decades of the 19th century. Louis Sullivan, in particular, created a style of ornamental motif in stone and terra cotta that showed reverence for the past artistry of classical embellishment, but he also expressed a fresh vitality and a new harmony between ornamentation and building design. His intricate lace-like interweaving style of patterns called guilloche had a strong flavor of Celtic imagery in its repetition and form. It also expressed a strong sense of the organic flow common to the emerging style Art Nouveau. Sullivan's façades were bold and heavily geometric, encrusted in rich decorative designs. He returned the use of the frieze to popularity, utilizing them in many commercial buildings. He also frequently employed enriched foliated motifs that often depicted scrolls of foliage, especially vines, called rinceau, in his work. Even along the jambs of doorways or entryways, he enriched spaces with foliated ornamentation. Sullivan's architectural style remains timeless and important because in it he did not so much apply decoration to his

Right: 19th century Italian carved stone bench with cherubs reclining with their wings forming the upper corners of the bench. The piece is fashioned in the classical tradition of ancient Rome with acanthus leaves forming the design motif for the legs and the stone slab of the seat carved to appear like a rolled cushion. The backrest carries the symmetrical lines of Neo-classicism. An emblem of Italian heraldic design is engraved on the backrest.

Carved stone bench
Italian, late 19th century.
Richard H. Driehaus Collection
1995

Left: Burnished red terra cotta fragment by George Grant Elmslie, proponent of the Prairie School of design, from about 1936, part of a larger frieze designed by him for the Olive Morton School in Hammond, Indiana. Elmslie executes this in the distinctive style made so popular by Chicago architects Louis Sullivan and Frank Lloyd Wright. Within the geometric symmetry a delicate touch of the Art Nouveau and Arts and Crafts movement merging with the Art Deco can be seen in this most original American style.

Right: Cast concrete sculpture, "A Sculpture," by artist Carl Beil, circa 1908–1909, from the artist's studio.

buildings as make them an integral part of the buildings themselves. His remarkable design of the Chicago Stock Exchange (now gone), for instance, set a high standard for refined urban architecture. The extraordinary design motif lavishly expressed in its exuberant stone cornice was repeated and carried through the building in the designs for its bronze elevator grates and in his ornate stenciling of the exchange's trading room (reassembled now at the Chicago Art Institute). Sullivan's ornamentation added a powerful layer of civility to the changing terrain of urban architecture. Today, more than a century later, his work remains fresh and modern. His ornamentation is still understated and aesthetically pleasing to the eye. Sullivan spent his life attempting not so much to eliminate ornament, but rather to discover ornament that was appropriate to the modern age. His work is America's most lasting and expressive interpretation of Art Nouveau and his "form follows function" credo remains the lasting law of modern design. His work was imbued with a unique sensitivity to architecture's human function. Underneath the beauty and grandeur of Sullivan's expressive style was a deep and inventive utility that understood the need of man for aesthetically pleasing surroundings. For him being free from clutter did not necessarily mean from decorative embellishment.

His influence on a generation of architects and artists was substantial. In the designs of such other American architects as George Elmslie (Sullivan's chief draftsman), the hallmark of the Chicago School's simplicity and style lived on. Elmslie's work, particularly in terra cotta, remains an outstanding expression of modern design. It is very reminiscent of Sullivanesque style. His rich, encrusted foliated patterns of ornament, both interior and exterior, continued the Chicago School's move toward highly modern design. Richard E. Schmidt, another Chicago School influenced architect, who specialized in unique commercial building design, as well as domestic architecture, also demonstrates that lace-like ornamentation in the stonework of his building. In 1915 he designed the main building for Chicago's Cook County Hospital, soon to be slated for demolition. This huge titanic of a building is thick with ornamental stone and terra cotta designs.

Frank Lloyd Wright also acknowledged the influence of Sullivan upon his work. In his austere but tranquil ornamentation, Wright often echoes the linear imagery that was so much a part of Sullivan's style. The geometric and organic nature of Wright's designs is also reminiscent of that restrained and patterned ornamental form.

Left: The front entrance of a David Adler designed house in Lake Forest, Illinois. Based on a house the architect knew from Versailles, it is a regal amber brick mansion with very high ceilings and extraordinary symmetrical lines. Here, a limestone Bacchus, the god of grain, left, and a limestone Ceres, the goddess of wheat, right, stand guard near the shore of Lake Michigan.

Right: A dramatic urban garden. The gnarled dwarf Cypress tree and Virginia Creeper encircle the artifacts of old Chicago. Two roundles from the old Garrick Theater hang on the wall to the left, while two small cathroid columns with the figures of women are 19th century. In the foreground is a piece of terra cotta by Louis Sullivan.

Today, the ornamental designs of each of these architects—Sullivan, Elmslie, Schmidt, and Wright can be found with some consistency, salvaged and in pieces ranging in size from monumental to fit in the back seat of your car size. Both stone and terra cotta ornamentation turn up following the sad but inevitable destruction of a building or home of their designs.

With the advent of the Art Deco movement in the 1920s in the United States, stone ornamentation received fresh interest as a modern form. With the stunning expression of its simple but imaginative artistic modernity in such dramatic buildings as New York's Rockefeller Center,

Chicago's Board of Trade, and Chicago Stadium (now torn down), a highly stylized form appeared. When the U.S. Government sponsored work relief programs during the Great Depression of the 1930s, countless Art Deco works in stone appeared at post offices, government office buildings, bridges, and federal courthouses, giving artists work and the country a taste for avant-garde ornamentation. Now, more than seven decades later, it is not difficult to discover examples of this refreshing style available as urban growth and development reconfigure a building's use or large panels of such Art Deco friezes find their way to the market place.

The Ins and Outs and Dos and Don'ts of Successful Salvage Hunting

1. Keep at it. Finding what you want takes time. The salvage search isn't like buying a tie or a pair of golf shoes. It is more like buying a car. Browsing is important. Get to know the merchandise that is available in your area. Learn what is unavailable in your area or what particular salvage centers rarely stock. There is a good reason they don't carry some things.

2. Bring your own measuring tape. They are at a premium in most salvage centers.

3. Most purchases are final. Remember that.

4. If you are having something shipped, you usually have to deal directly with the freight company on big items.

5. The Internet has an abundance of web sites for salvage and reclamation centers. If the sites on the following pages don't turn anything up go to a big search engine and put in "Architectural Salvage," or the item that you are interested in, like "Cast Iron Urns." You will be surprised at the abundance of what you will discover.

6. Consider purchasing a "splurge" piece like a great stone column, a fireplace mantel, or a wondrous chandelier that will anchor the artistic style of your home. Then work around it.

7. Take the "Oath to Urban Eclecticism." Flee the pretensions of middle-class order and the need to propagate neat suburban conventions. Don't be afraid to embrace the artistic disorder of old refined aestheticism.

8. Don't be afraid to mix styles and periods. Neo-classical columns do work with Art Deco chrome sconces and ecclesiastical embellishments.

Below: The detail of this White French garden chair flows from its distinctive geometric design and whimsical shape that almost echoes "Ooh-la-la."

9. Learn to love or at least appreciate rust. It is usually an enhancement to any item worthy of having it. Rust is nature's way of adding to the beauty of iron. The distressed patina is a work of art.

10. Write down the dimensions of important areas of your home. Know what size ceiling you have; the height and width of doorframes; fireplace opening; and window size.

11. Go back to look at things again and again and again. Schmooze the dealer. Stocks shift, move, return, and change at different rates. Have a second and third look. But if you see something you really want and love, don't be foolish, buy it right away. The turn over in stock is sometimes done at a snail's pace, and then sometimes it is lightening quick. If you need something, buy it when first you discover it.

12. Learn to appreciate and adapt. Be creative. Alter the placement and use of certain grand items to spice up your environment. For instance, buy a nice glass chandelier that is not too expensive and then don't rewire it. Instead stick candles in it and hang it in your yard or patio.

13. Experiment. Find a marble bust. Put it in your bathtub and let it delight you when you shower. Maybe you can find a stone pedestal to put it on.

14. Use everything you buy. Take the bust out of the bathtub and put it in the middle of your dinner table and surround it with the other treasures you pick up. Eat around it. Use lots of candles and maybe you'll get a shadow of the bust on your wall. If you buy lanterns, don't just use them in the yard or garden. They are perfect too on your dinner table. Use everything. You can't clutter a table too much. Remember the oath you took.

15. When you go to salvage centers dress appropriately. You can easily tear your Prada dress on a wire chair. It happens. Wear clothes you can soil and repair.

16. Ask questions when you go to salvage centers. Ask the staff what they think. Most of them are nurturing folk. They really do want you to know what you are doing.

Above: These rich green-blue and clear glass electrical insulators add a distinctive touch of techno-artistry and appear nothing like they do in the everyday world of capping electrical lines on the countless electric poles across the country. However, these sturdy glass containers have many uses from candleholders to unusual beverage containers or ice cream dishes.

17. Have a special notebook or steno pad handy to record the things you see or are considering. You will be very glad to look back on the information you have gathered. Don't just trust your memory to keep track of merchandise to which you are attracted.

18. Remember you can't be too kooky!

19. If you find out you really do have bad taste, get help! Find someone you know and trust to help you. If you want to tie bows on everything or spray everything you buy with Rustoleum, be aware of the danger signals.

20. Buy books about art, architecture, and design. They will deepen your knowledge and also make excellent object d'arts. They can be stacked in piles, adding much grace to any room. Remember Jackie Kennedy's book cluttered bedroom on Fifth Avenue.

21. Buy an anchor piece of reclaimed architecture that will become the center of your vision. It might be a Regency gilt mirror (don't hang it stand it against the wall or on a mantelpiece); a wooden art screen; a French wire birdcage; a large factory table; some Parisian café chairs; or an iron bed to stick in your garden.

22. Be confident in the aesthetic beauty of each and every piece you purchase and bring home. If they have artistic value in their design and good lines they will work. Even if they are broken.

23. Own a pie safe.

24. No matter what you have it will always look better if you can find a gilt or stone acanthus leaf to sit near it. They are the emblems of classical nobility.

25. Buy and use a child's chair. If you don't have a child, put a napkin on the seat and use it to serve bread rolls at the dinner table.

26. Use multiple chandeliers in the same room.

27. You can't have too many mirrors. Put big mirrors in small rooms.

28. Don't be afraid to appear eccentric. It is a mark of good breeding and taste. If you hate the rusted distressed condition of white aged French garden furniture go to Kmart and buy plastic.

29. Try to see things not only as they look in front of you at the salvage center, but also as they might look surrounded by your other treasures. I don't mean, "How does the pedestal look with the iron stove." I mean, you have the glass chandelier. You see the large heavy wrought iron French parrott cage holder. Now—can you see the chandelier hanging from the iron holder?

30. Remember every item has at least four uses. First the one for which it was made. Then there are two that only you will figure out when you get home. Then there is the one that will only come after you live with some piece. Perhaps that will be when you move the French doors from the dining room to the lawn.

31. Don't forget that nature doesn't always ruin indoor things outdoors. Rain, snow, sun, and chilly winds won't harm stone, glass, cast iron, glass, or wood. Do more outdoor thinking. Put the stone corbel outside. Bring the urns inside. Ring your rooms with them.

32. Don't forget the bathroom. Be creative. That tall pedestal urn might be perfect for conversion into a bathroom sink.

33. Break up the set. You're not your grandmother. Your chairs don't need to match. Having twelve for dinner? How about twelve different kinds of chairs. Gothic. Arts and Craft. Deco. Café. Modern. Fancy. Plain. Keep your eyes peeled for ecclesiastical furniture. Mixing is good.

34. Remember the formula for seating groups. 2 pedestals + one door = one funky picnic bench.

35. Use your brain. If you can learn the names of five imported beers, you can learn and remember the names of the five types of classical Greek and Roman columns. Bass, Guinness, Beck's, St. Pauli Girl, and Dos Equis. Doric, Ionic, Corinthian, Tuscan, and Composite. See?

36. Remember that architecture is art just as much as any painting or statue. An urn has artistic value just like a David Hockney, Caravaggio, or Jackson Pollock. Someone made it. Hopefully with their hands and heart.

37. Fashions and tastes change. Mostly as reactions against past influences of history and excesses of designs. Learn what sets a piece in the context of its time. It will provide you with the layers of meaning and heritage.

Above: Clock faces are great for decoration and can be used to create interesting effects almost anywhere.

Web Sites

Websites in America & Canada

www.adamandevesalvage.com
Filled with antiques and interesting items salvaged from contemporary homes to castles in cities far and near. An Online catalogue that includes tiles and baths, gates and fencing, garden features, and more. Based in Palm Beach, Florida.

www.adkinsantiques.com
Discover salvaged architectural artifacts and embellishments for the home and garden at Adkins Architectural Antiques. The website offers a variety of items including artefacts, doors, hardware, and lighting. Restoration and custom work done on premises. Based in Texas.

www.aoarchitecturalsalvage.com
Based in Kansas City, Missouri, this site is a haven for Antiques and Oddities. A vast range of salvage items including stained glass, iron, lamps and lighting, columns, doors, hardware, mantels, and many more.

www.architecturalsalvage.com
From their large inventory of lighting, mantels, entryways, and backbars, you can choose from a constant stock of unusual items. They specialize in reproduction mahogany entryways with leaded glass, but also offer a diverse assortment of antiques including pool tables, door hardware, sinks and plumbing fixtures, stained glass, armoires, pedestals, statuary, ceramics and pottery, chimney tops, chairs, tables, stonework, weathervanes, ironwork, and much more. Unique yard and garden items such as terra cotta, iron gates, fountains, and outdoor furnishings are also available. Situated in Kentucky.

www.architectural-salvage.com
Home of Crescent City Architecturals, New Orleans. Specialists in saving, salvaging, and recycling the past for you.

www.architecturalsalvagevt.com
Based in Burlington, VT, this site features mantels, doors, windows,hardware, plumbing, and more. Architectural antiques are available at warehouse, by e-mail or phone.

www.ashevillearchitectural.com
Home of Asheville Architectural Salvage and Antiques, North Carolina. The site contains unique architectural treasures to give your home old house charm, or to help make your restoration project more authentic.

www.churchclearinghouse.com
Offers to purchase furnishings, and maintains an inventory of items that may appeal to clients designing and furnishing churches. Currently operating in the USA.

www.driftwoodsalvage.com
Whole House Building Supply and Salvage website. Based in California, they offer quality building materials that have been donated or salvaged from area homes and businesses.

www.fifisalvage.com
(Finally I found It Salvage) Specializes in antiques and architectural salvage pieces, located in Maine.

www.greatsalvage.com
An Architectural Salvage Warehouse. Situated in Vermont, they specialize in mantels, doors, windows, plumbing, lighting and much, much more.

www.historictile.com
The Historic Tile and European Reclamation website. Specializing in the importation of European architectural salvage over 100 years old. Based in North America.

www.homesupply.com
Historic home supply Corp. An architectural salvage company based in New York. Offer a vast collection of unique and old housewares. www.housewreckers.com – House Wreckers, based in USA. Many salvaged items from historic homes and estates including doors, windows, tubs, toilets, wrought iron, sinks, mantels and many, many more.

www.legacyofmpls.com
Legacy Architectural Salvage Gallery of Minneapolis – Offers architectural antiques including doors, lighting fixtures, stained glass windows, plumbing, masonry.

www.ohmegasalvage.com
Ohmega Salvage are committed to preserving the architectural heritage of the Bay Area. They buy and sell usual and unusual building materials. They have made their mark in the Bay Area over the last 20 years as the leading Supplier of restoration materials to architects, contractors, and homeowners.

www.oldegoodthings.com
Specializing in American architectural antiques such as mantels, doorknobs & hardware, decorative iron, iron & wood furniture, stones & terra cotta, mirrors, flooring, and more. Based in New York.

www.oldhouseparts.com
Focuses on 18th, 19th, and early 20th century architectural artifacts and salvage. They will also assist customers in finding unique pieces for individual restorations.

www.oldhousesalvage.com
Dealer of original old house salvage – from antique hardware to entrance ways, mantles, clawfoot tubs, marble sinks, and windows. Based in New Hampshire.

www.omegatoo.com
Specializing in fine antique and vintage-style lighting and plumbing fixtures, miscellaneous hardware, and decorative accessories. Based in Berkeley, California.

www.onewayarchitecturalantiques.com
One Way, based in North Carolina, believes strongly in salvaging our past and recycling and thus honoring the craftsmen who would other-

wise be forgotten. Offering a unique collection of wrought iron, terra cotta, rocks and more.

www.portlandsalvage.com
Seeks to meet the market demand for architectural salvage pieces by buying as well as selling a vast range of pieces. Based in Maine.

www.recyclingthepast.com
Company based in New Jersey, specializing in architectural salvage and antiques from around the USA. An eclectic variety of treasures such as architectural antiques, mantles, stained glass windows, lighting fixtures, iron gates, and fencing. All carefully chosen for their authenticity and uniqueness.

www.salvageone.com
Source for architectural salvage with 100,000 square feet of 18th through to 20th century architectural furnishings for the home and garden, situated in Chicago.

www.salvageweb.com
A useful directory site providing information to salvage businesses and homeowners.

www.seacoastsalvage.com
Based in Rockland, ME, Seacoast Salvage locates and recycles architectural elements, parts of houses and other buildings.

www.seattlebuildingsalvage.com
Antique and vintage building fixtures salvage, restoration and reproduction including lighting, doors, bath, windows, and other hardware and house parts stemming from Seattle.

www.steptoes.com.au
Web site of Steptoe's Restoration Supplies, in Victoria, Canada. Specializes in original period pieces rescued from demolition of old churches, houses, public and commercial buildings. They also provide a restoration and repair service.

www.thesummerbeam.com
Dealer of architectural antiques and historic wood, promising to bring history in to your home. Based in Seattle.

www.timberandstone.com
Located in Fredericksburg, TX. Specializes in restoration of original pioneer buildings that range from 100 to 200 years old. In many cases entire history of cabin can be provided.

www.urbanartifacts.net
At the forefront of rescuing tin and architectural objects throughout the United States, Urban Artifacts operate through 2000 retailers across the country. Their headquarters are based in Wisconsin.

www.vermontsalvage.com
Buyers and sellers of doors, windows, plumbing and other forms of architectural salvage taken from old buildings.

www.vintagebeamsandtimbers.com
"Building the future by reclaiming the past." Vintage Beams and Timber Inc. are a multi-faceted company based in North Carolina, supplying fine recycled and antique lumber to the United States.

Websites in UK & Ireland

www.angelarchitectural.com
Angel Architectural caters for architectural decoration and heritage requirements. They offer garden statuary, patio cast iron, wrought iron garden furniture, doors and window furniture, columns, gates, chimney pots, fireplaces of wood and marble and cast iron. All types of brass embellishment, bronzes, lighting, sun dials, barometers, clocks etc. Experts in the field of restoration and refurbishment of fireplaces. Based in Co. Limerick, Ireland.

www.antiquepubbars.com
They offer bars, and other architectural features, with splendid reclaimed antique elements. Use of fine antique carved wood, stained glass, cut mirrors, marble and tiles, to create features with styles from Jacobean, Victorian through to Art Deco, fashioned to your preference. Based in Burnley, UK.

www.architectural-salvage.co.uk
All around valuable site offering, among many things, a fireplace restoration and marble cleaning service. Company based in Co. Durham, UK.

www.borders-architectural.com
Based in Northumberland, England, it stocks a large range of garden antiques, including urns, seats and benches, troughs and griffins. Also a vast spectrum of doors, fireplaces, and period chimney pieces.

www.catbrain.com
Website of the Minchinhampton Architectural Salvage company – dealers in original and bespoke architectural items, garden ornaments and decorative elements. Located in the heart of the English Cotswolds.

www.cheshirebrickandslate.co.uk
Cheshire Brick & Slate Company, a well established organization in Cheshire, England. A comprehensive web site offering all salvage elements as well as landscaping, demolition, and reclamation teams.

www.drummonds-arch.co.uk
Web site of Drummonds Architectural Antiques Ltd. Based in Surrey, England, they offer a vast array of salvage elements to cater for all tastes and future projects.

www.easy-arch-salv.co.uk
Web site of the Edinburgh Arhitectural Salvage Yards. Containing everything from times past; Georgian, Victorian, Art Nouveau through to Art Deco.

www.global-reclamation.co.uk
Global Reclamation Ltd. are based in Nottingham, England and supply reclaimed oak timbers, beams, hardwood flooring, and general architectural building materials.

www.handr.co.uk
Hulton & Rostron's web site. Based in Surrey, UK, allows people to find, buy, sell, and exchange architectural and landscape features and materials through the aid of an online electronic forum.

www.lassco.co.uk
LASSCO (The London Architectural Salvage & Supply Co.) is London's largest, best known, and longest established architectural antiques and salvage company. It comprises five specialist shops based at three central London sites. Specializes in architectural antiques and salvage including fireplaces, mantels, stained glass, and garden ornaments.

www.olliffs.com
Olliff's architectural antiques – trader in Architectural antiques, antique garden ornaments, and reclaimed building materials, based in the UK.

www.originalfeatures.co.uk
Specializes in supplying and installing products for the restoration of 19th and early 20th century properties. Based in London, UK.

www.tynemoutharchitecturalsalvage.com
UK company described as "an Aladdin's Cave full of original features." Tynemouth Architectural Salvage is a mass of reclaimed stock from all eras and parts of the world.

www.victorian-salvage.com
The Victorian Salvage & Joinery Company Ltd., in Ireland. They travel all over Europe to bring you the finest in stone, timber, and wood and have a large collection of doors, architronics, and mouldings covering Georgian to Edwardian periods.

Glossary

Acanthus: A large voluptuous leafy herbaceous plant found in the Mediterranean area whose organic scalloped beauty became a popular decorative motif used by the Romans. Corinthian columns are ornamented with the rich application of Acanthus leaves.

American Victorian: An architectural style popularized in America during the second half of the 19th century that marked a transition from the earlier tastes for Greek Revival fashion.

Architecture: The art of building design and construction.

Arts and Crafts: A 19th century artistic style that longed for a return to hand-made items of quality and artistry, rejecting the shabby products of industrial mass production. It was also a reaction to the clutter and eclecticism of Victorian fashion.

Art Deco: A highly modern architectural style that flourished at the start of the 20th century and became emblematic of the 1920s and 1930s with lots of chrome and simple gray stone. Think "Chrysler Building."

Art Glass: Decoratively fashioned colored glass used to embellish windows.

Art Nouveau: A distinctive style of architectural design that featured an organic style of ornamentation at the end of the 19th century that was synonymous with fin de siecle French modern tastes that gave the world a reason to use olive, lilac, violet, and sage green colors in domestic interiors. Think "Maxine's."

Above: Yellow leather and Japanese maple chairs designed by Frank Lloyd Wright for use in the dining room of his landmark Imperial Hotel in Tokyo, Japan.

Baluster: A vertical ornamental post that supports the railing of a staircase.

Balustrade: A series of balusters that form the support railing of a staircase or of an ornamental railing, usually stone, decorating a roof in many 18th and 19th century houses.

Base: The bottom of a column.

Belevedere: A structure built to overlook or view a garden panorama.

Botanicals: Plants, flowers, and blooming things.

Bracket: A horizontal support that holds an overhead weight such as a shelf or an ornamental corbel.

Cantilevered: A projecting beam secured at only one end.

Capital: The carved or molded head of a column.

Caryatid: A column in the form of a female figure.

Casement Window: A window that is hinged to the window frame and opens by swinging out on its side.

Cast Iron: A commercial alloy of iron, carbon, and silicon that is cast in a mold and is hard, brittle, and nonmalleable.

Clerestory: Windows near the ceiling in a high room or hall that receive light from above the roofs of adjoining buildings.

Closed-string: A type of stairway in which the balusters are set into the string, the rising diagonal support that runs up the side of the stairs, instead of the steps.

Chandelier: A light fixture permitting the use of multiple candles or lights that is made with extravagant glass and crystal beading and teardrops that amplified the power of the lights.

Chevron: A zig-zag pattern used in Medieval architecture.

Commercial: Salvage that comes from the material and equipment of restaurants and businesses. Usually small in scale and practical in nature, such as barber chairs, doctor tables, and tavern bars.

Dentils: A series of small block-like ornaments resembling teeth used as part of a frieze or cornice made popular in Georgian period homes and also appearing in revival styles.

Double-hung windows: A window with two movable vertical framed panes, one upper and one

lower, capable of sliding up and down on tracks by a system of counterweights concealed within the window casing.

Eclectic: The mixing of a variety of styles and sources of ornament and design.

Edwardian: An era of architectural and design style that emerged after the Victorian age during the reign of King Edward VII that sought to simplify some of the overdone fashions of the 19th century. It was an expression of longing for more modern styles.

Entablature: The horizontal beam that is supported by a classical column.

Façade: The face of a building. What you see standing in front of a building.

Fanlight: A semicircular non-opening ornamental window above a door with wood or cast iron muntins (frame) securing segmented glass panes, resembling an unfurled fan and popularized in late 18th century houses.

Federal Style: American architectural style popular between 1780 and 1820.

Firedog: A container or device which is used to hold fuel such as wood or coal in a fireplace.

Finial: A small decorative device used on the tops of newel posts, roofs, furniture, or piers. A geometric ornament, heavily carved, or rendered to look like an urn or an orb. Very popular in 18th century architecture.

Folly: An architectural form or building designed to add elegance and grace to a view or panorama with little regard to its practical utility that was fashionable on great country estates in the 18th century. Connolly's Folly at Castletown House in County Kildare, Ireland, is a fine example of a thundering architectural creation with no other objective but to be seen from a distance.

French Door: A set of two matched doors with rectangular panels of glass.

Frieze: The central section of the entablature of a building, just below the cornice area in which the roof meets the wall. An area in the architecture of Classical antiquity that often received high sculptural embellishment representing mythic figures or stories.

Gargoyle: A rain or water spout on a medieval building that directs water away from the walls of the building carved with grotesque representations of the heads of beasts.

Georgian Style: English period of architecture and design between 1714 and 1837 which reflected the restrained proportions and linear form of Ancient

Greece and Rome and flourished during the reigns of Kings George I, George II, George III, George IV, and, residually, William IV, until Queen Victoria came to the throne.

Greek Revival: An architectural style very popular in American from 1825 until 1860 that reflected the buildings of ancient Greece. Many resembled Greek Temples. Many of the elegant plantations of the American South were designed in this style before the Civil War.

Greek Temple: A Classical revival architectural building, modeled on those of ancient Greece, usually a domed structure with columns that became fashionable in the 18th century.

Handrail: The horizontal support atop the balusters of a stairway that in addition to forming a balustrade, provides a device to hold when ascending and descending the stairway.

Hoodmold: An ornamental decoration usually placed above an exterior window.

Industrial: Salvage that is the material and equipment from factories and manufacturing plants. Burley and technical elements and devices usually of a refined engineering and technology, such as industrial lighting fixtures and lathe machines.

Italianate: A style of architecture popularized between 1840 and 1885 and whose Italian Villa shape dominated American architecture.

Jamb: The side of a door, window, or an arch.

Lintel: A load bearing element above a window or a door, often a long rectilinear stone or wooden beam.

Mansard Roof: A roof with two slopes, one being almost vertical, that permits the use of interior roof space. Popularized first in Paris during the Second Empire, it was a style named after its French architect and used heavily in Italianate and Queen Anne architecture in America.

Modern: An architectural style of stark un-embellished simplicity utilizing a bare-bones glass and steel form of construction that became popular in the decades after World War II and influenced the shape of many cities in an explosion of urban architecture. Fostered by such architects as Ludwig Mies Van der Rohe and Phillip Johnson.

Molding: A contoured ornamental strip or decorative band providing a transitional frame between one surface and another, particularly between a ceiling and walls, or surrounding windows or doors.

Mullion: A vertical supporting bar between windowpanes or the panels of a door.

Muntin: The pieces forming and securing the small segments of a multiple paned window.

Newel: A post located at the bottom and top of a stairway connecting to the railing and banister providing support.

Nosing: The front edge of a stair. The lip that hangs over.

Open-string: A type of stairway design in which the balusters are set directly into the step.

Oriel Window: A window that projects out from the exterior wall of a building and extends out over ground.

Ornamentation: The nonstructural elements of a building's decoration that assist in its beautification and embellishment of design.

Pattern Book: A book of architectural detail and design based on the revival principals of Classical architecture that popularized the style by enabling engineers and architects to copy the plans of Classical design.

Pediment: An Classical architectural embellishment used above door or window surrounds, often triangular in form.

Pergola: A decorative garden arbor formed of a trellis supported on posts.

Pie Safe: A small vented cabinet, usually tin, to keep fresh baked pies free of flies and small children.

Pilaster: A flat decorative pier, a two-dimensional column-like architectural embellishment, often with a capital and base, popularly used with door surrounds in the 18th and 19th centuries.

Pointed Arch: A frequently used element of Gothic architecture in which arches form a point at its apex. Used with great frequency in church and cathedral doorways and in ecclesiastical windows and other design motifs.

Portico: A roofed, columned walkway or covered element of design. A porch open on one or more sides formed by columns. Used in Georgian, Federal, and Greek Revival architecture.

Prairie: A style of American architectural design that began in the early decades of the 20th century and was made popular by Chicago architect Frank Lloyd Wright. It expressed elements of the Arts and Craft movement in a uniquely modern American heartland manner.

Proportion: The balanced relationship between the dimensions of size, form, and shape.

Quatrefoil: An opening carved into four leaf-shaped foils used in Gothic architecture.

Quions: A Georgian architectural design feature in which oversized stone blocks are inserted into the brick ends of a façade creating a decorative pattern rising up the height of the walls.

Reclaimed Architecture: An element of architectural design formerly used for one purpose or function that is reused for the sake of its intrinsic ornamental beauty or its continued practical utility.

Riser: The vertical portion of a stair. The back part you do not walk on.

Rococo: A very elaborate style of ornamentation in the late Georgian period. A swing in tastes from the radical simplicity of early Georgian styles that demonstrates an evolution in 18th century fashions.

Salvage: The saving of an element of architectural design or beauty.

Sash: The framework of a window that supports its glass.

Sconce: A wall fixture of one or more candles or lights suitable for high embellished ornamentation.

Shaft: The main part of a column.

Scullery: The area of a kitchen or the outer room of a kitchen where pots and pans are cleaned and stored.

Shutters: Exterior devices of planked wood protecting interiors from the outside elements. Interior shutters, often louvered, permitted some control of air-flow and sunlight within domestic interiors.

Sill: Horizontal element at the bottom of a window or a door.

String: The diagonal support portion of a stairway running up along the side of the stairway.

Symmetry: The balance and proportion of a shape or form, corresponding in size and the arrangement of parts.

Terra Cotta: Italian for "baked earth," reddish-brown clay that is easily molded, baked, and often glazed. Highly utilitarian, practical, and inexpensive.

Tracery: Ornamental carving of mullions and transoms in Gothic windows.

Trefoil: An opening carved into three leaf-shaped foils used in Gothic architecture.

Transom: A window above a door which permits natural light to enter hallways, rooms, and entryways.

Tread: The horizontal surface of a stair. The part you walk on.

Urn: A garden receptacle of Classical origins based on the designs of a Greek and Roman antiquity employing a cup shape (tazza) and a bell shape (Campana).

Vernacular: A style of architecture that arises from popular traditions or tastes that emphasizes the practical utility or more functional simplification of certain styles. Usually this means the adaptation of an architectural style.

Veranda: A large covered wrap around porch or balcony whose roof is often supported by columns. The style was highly popular in the American South in the era before the Civil War.

Victorian: A era of architecture and design during the long reign of Britain's Queen Victoria from 1837 until her death in 1901. During this period the industrial age came to full flourish with most inventiveness and progress.

Bibliography and Index

Bartlett, Apple Parish and Susan Bartlett Crater. *Sister, the Life of the Legendary American Interior Decorator, Mrs. Henry Parish II.* New York: St. Martins Press, 2000.

Burdick, John. *American Colonial Homes, A Pictorial History.* Philadelphia: Courage Books, 1998.

Churchill, Henrietta Spencer. *Classic Georgian Style.* New York: Collins & Brown, 1997.

Fitzgerald, Olda. *Irish Gardens.* New York: Hearst, 1999.

Halliday, Stephen. *The Great Stink of London, Sir Joseph Bazalgette and the Cleansing of the Victorian Capital.* London: Sutton Publishing, 1999.

Innes, Miranda. *The Fireplace Book.* New York: Viking, 2000.

Israel, Barbara. *Antique Garden Ornament, Two Centuries of American Taste.* New York: Harry N. Abrams, Inc., 1999.

Jackson-Stops, Gervasse and James Pipkin. *The English Country House, A Grand Tour.* Boston: Little, Brown & Company, 1985.

Keno, Leigh and Leslie Keno. *Hidden Treasures, Searching for Masterpieces of American Furniture.* New York: Warner Books, 2000.

Lovatt-Smith, Lisa. *Paris Interiors.* Koln: Taschen, 1994.

McBride, Simon and Karen Howes. *Private Ireland, Irish Living and Irish Style Today.* New York: St. Martin's Press, 1999.

Miller, Judith. *More Period Details, the House Renovators Bible.* New York: Clarkson Potter, 1999.

Morrow, Ann. *Picnic in a Foreign Land, the Eccentric Lives of the Anglo-Irish.* London: Grafton, 1989.

O'Brien, Jacqueline, and Guinness, Desmond. *Great Irish Houses and Castles.* London, Weidenfeld & Nicolson, Ltd., 1993.

Ruthven, Ianthe. *The Irish Home, Eclectic and Unique Interiors.* New York: Rizzoli, 1998.

Seebohm, Caroline, and Christopher Simon-Sykes, *English Country, Living in England's Private Houses.* New York: Clarkson N. Potter, 1987.

Somerville-Large, Peter. *The Irish Country House, A Social History.* London: Sinclair Stevenson, 1995.

The Treasures of Britain, and the Treasures of Ireland. London: Drive Publications, Ltd., 1972.

Varney, Carlton. *Drapper Touch, the High Life and High Style of Dorothy Drapper.* New York, Prentiss Hall Press, 1988.

Vreeland, Diana. *D. V.* New York: Alfred A. Knoph, 1984.

Yenne, Bill. *Gothic Gargoyles.* New York: Barnes & Nobel Books, 2000.

Ypma, Herbert. *Irish Georgian.* London: Thames & Hudson, 1998.

Acknowledgements and Credits

I am grateful to all those whose kindness, expertise, and hospitality helped to give depth and beauty to this book. To those who opened their homes, salvage centers, gardens, their studios, schools, and restaurants, I am indebted. You have been generous with your laughter, loveliness, and ease.

Master gardener, collector, and raconteur Mark Steinke of Salvage One, for his wise collaboration and wit; Hon. Edward M. and Hon. Anne M. Burke; Margaret Dargan; Joe Beale and his associates at the Hotel Allegro, Chicago; the wonderful staff of Salvage One who did so much heavy lifting with both brain and brawn - John de Koker; Breckenridge Armstrong III; John Hetzel; Moni Janis; Shemek Drabio; Louis Nieves and Davide Nanni (sculptor extraordinaire). Scott Filar of Mad Parade; Deborah Coleman of Pavilion; John Chandler, Rev. Brian Paulson, S.J., Ron Mangan and the Administration of St. Ignatius College Prep in Chicago; Richard Norton of Richard Norton Inc; Fernando Lopez of Settimana Restaurant; resauranteur Jerry Kleiner; Margaret Lundquist; Jane O'Neil; and other anonymous gardening grandees; the erudite Seymour Perskey, a devoted collector and student of Louis Sullivan and Frank Lloyd Wright; Columnist and designer Jonathan Wells; Chicago attorney Martin Dolan; Billy Hoffman; Joseph Gramacki; Matt Link; Lindy Fleming; Jack Brown and the staff of the Burnham-Ryerson Library of the Art Institute of Chicago; Commissioner Mary Dempsey and the staff of the Chicago Public Library; Karen Skubish, Karen Smith and the staff of the Newberry Library of Chicago; Mark and Mary Beth Bowman; Gordon St. George Mark; Rose Marie O'Neill; Hon. Desmond Guinness; The Knight of Glin and Madame Olda Fitzgerald and the Irish Georgian Society; John Dombrowski and Victoria Dal Santo; Benjamin and Stacey Mednick; the late Lady Caroline Blackwood. And to generations of O'Connors who refined my eyes to appreciate beauty and O'Gormans who gave me the wits to write of it.

Very special thanks to my editor, Martin Howard; master photographer Simon Clay; and photo editor Louise Daubeny whose companionship and thoughtful collaboration became half the fun of working on this project.

The publisher wishes to thank Simon Clay for taking all the photography in this book, with the following exceptions:

Richard Waite/Arcaid for page 2
Alan Weintraub/Arcaid for pages 9, 10, 12, 58-59, 80, 93, 97, 104, 109, 130-131, 141, 146-147, 152 and 153
Chrysalis Images for pages 19, 20, 21, 22, 23, 24, 25, 28, 29, 34, 35, 36, 37, 39, 40, 41, 52 and 53
© Bob Krist/CORBIS for page 26
© Stephanie Maze/CORBIS for page 27
© Philippa Lewis/CORBIS for page 30
© Mark E. Gibson/CORBIS for page 31
© Clay Perry/CORBIS for pages 32 and 44
© Jerry Tubby/CORBIS for page 33
© Massimo Listri/CORBIS for page 38
© Stefano Bianchetti/CORBIS for page 42
© Marko Modic/CORBIS for page 43
© Michael Boys/CORBIS for page 45
© Richard Schulman/CORBIS for page 46
© Rodney Hyett/CORBIS for page 47
© CORBIS for pages 48, 49, 50 and 51
Richard Bryant/Arcaid for pages 105, 135 (top left) and 138
Premium/Arcaid 112 (left)
© Marianne Haas/CORBIS for page 116
© Michael Freeman/CORBIS for page 117
© Tommy Candler/CORBIS for page 119
© Michael Nicholson/CORBIS for page 120
Jeremy Cockayne/Arcaid for page 128